CZECHOSLOVAKIA

Profile of a
Socialist Republic
at the Crossroads of Europe

NATIONS OF CONTEMPORARY EASTERN EUROPE

CZECHOSLOVAKIA

Profile of a
Socialist Republic
at the Crossroads of Europe

David W. Paul

Westview Press / Boulder, Colorado

Nations of Contemporary Eastern Europe

Copyright © 1981 by Westview Press, Inc.

Published in 1981 in the United States of America by
        Westview Press, Inc.
        5500 Central Avenue
        Boulder, Colorado 80301
        Frederick A. Praeger, Publisher

Library of Congress Cataloging in Publication Data
Paul, David W.
        Czechoslovakia, profile of a Socialist republic at the crossroads of Europe.
        (Nations of contemporary Eastern Europe)
        Bibliography: p.
        Includes index.
        1. Czechoslovakia. I. Title. II. Series.
DB2011.P38   943.7   80-19333
ISBN 0-89158-861-2

Printed and bound in the United States of America

To my parents
with love
and appreciation

Contents

Tables and Figures

Photographs

Note on the Pronunciation of Czech and Slovak

Although Czech and Slovak are two separate languages, they are closely related members of the West Slavic language family and are governed by essentially the same rules of pronunciation. In both cases, the alphabet is quite phonetic, and therefore there is no ambiguity about the pronunciation of words and names. The accent invariably falls on the first syllable. Long vowels are marked with the symbol ´ and short vowels are unmarked. Thus, in the name *Novotný*, the mark over the final *y* indicates that that vowel is long; the accent falls on the first syllable, hence the name is pronounced NO-vot-nee. In general, vowels are sounded according to the continental pattern: *a* is pronounced as "ah" in English and simply held longer when marked *á*; *e* is spoken as it is in the English word "bet" when short, but approaches the sound of "ay" in "day" when long; *i* is close to its corresponding English letter in "bit," but it becomes *ee* as in "peel" when long; *o* is sounded rather like "aw" in "thaw" when short, but lengthened to an open "oh" when marked *ó*; *u* is close to the sound heard in "put," and long *ú* (marked *ů* in the middle or at the end of Czech words) is pronounced as the long *oo* in "boot"; *y* and *ý* are approximately equivalent to *i* and *í*. The combination *ou* is not a diphthong but rather requires the pronunciation of both vowels run somewhat together. The Slovak *ä* sounds approximately like short *e*.

Most consonants are pronounced approximately the way their English equivalents are spoken, with the following exceptions: (1) voiced consonants become unvoiced at the end of words (e.g., *b* at the end of a word is pronounced *p, d* is pronounced *t, v* becomes *f*); (2) *d, n,* and *t* appearing before the vowels *ě* and *i* (*í*) become softened and are pronounced similarly to their English equivalents in, for example, "ver*d*ure" and "*t*une." When *n* is marked *ň*, it also takes on this softness irrespective of the vowel that follows, as in the name *Chňoupek.* The same is true of the marked *d'* and *t'.* The following consonants are pronounced differently from their English counterparts: *c* = "ts" as in "cats"; *č* = "ch" as in "chair"; *ch* = Scottish "ch" as in "*loch*"; *j* = consonantal "y" as in "yes"; *r* is trilled with the tongue and, when marked *ř*, is pronounced simultaneously with the added sound of "zh" or "sh"; *š* = "sh" as in "shirt"; and *ž* = "zh" as in the word "leisure" or "azure."

Some examples:

Masaryk	is pronounced	MAH-sah-rick
Beneš	"	"	BEN-esh
Václav	"	"	VAHTS-lahf
Smrkovský	"	"	SMER*-kof-skee
Příbram	"	"	PRSHEE-brahm

*The *r* in Smrkovský thus serves as a "half-vowel" and is distinctly pronounced. The same is often true of *l*, as in Plzeň.

CZECHOSLOVAKIA

Profile of a
Socialist Republic
at the Crossroads of Europe

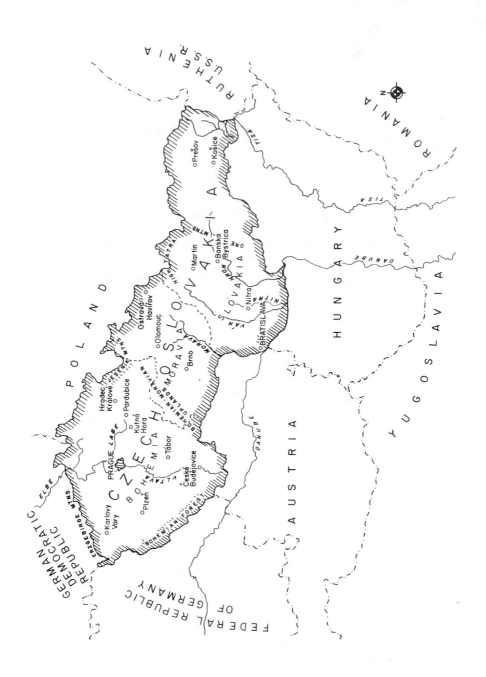

1

Historical Backgrounds

Czechoslovakia as a political entity did not come into being until 1918, but the lands comprising modern day Czechoslovakia have a rich history reaching back many centuries. The earliest records, such as they are, suggest that Celtic tribes inhabited much of the region sometime before the birth of Christ. It was from one of these tribes, the Boii, that the westernmost territories received the name Bohemia. Around 8 B.C. Germanic groups (Teutons) moved into the region of the Boii and pushed steadily eastward into Moravia (named after the Morava River, which flows through the region) and the area now called Slovakia. It is uncertain exactly when the first Slavic tribes made their appearance, but it may have been as early as the first century A.D. Slavs and Teutons alike were overrun by the Avars in the sixth century. Eventually, the Avars themselves were overthrown and destined for oblivion as a race. In the west, they were defeated early in the seventh century by the most powerful of the Slavic groups in the region, the Czechs, who were able to subjugate other peoples in the area as well. Farther east, the Avars held onto their territories until a final defeat by the armies of Charlemagne (c. 796).

During the next half-century there arose a state centering in Moravia, at first a fiefdom of Charlemagne's empire and later a united kingdom under the rule of a Slavic prince, Mojmir I (c. 818–c. 846). His successors, Rastislav and Svätopluk, expanded the domains of Moravia to include Bohemia, southern Poland, modern-day Slovakia, and western Hungary. This expanded kingdom became known as the Great Moravian Empire.

Although Svätopluk's empire was a sizable domain in its time, many details of its approximately one-hundred-year existence are the subject of historical debate. For a long time, modern historians apparently confused the Moravian Empire with a city by the same name (Morava) located far to the south in Pannonia. Thus there is some doubt as to exactly how the empire related to other political units of the Middle Ages, when and under what circumstances Christianity was spread throughout the empire, and many similarly important questions.[1]

In any event, following Svätopluk's death in 894 the empire was weakened by disputes among the great ruler's three sons and by the interference of the East Frankish king, Arnulf. In this condition, Moravia fell victim to new invaders, the Magyar (Hungarian) tribes, which conquered and destroyed the Moravian empire in 907 and secured Hungarian control over the eastern regions for the next one thousand years. The Kingdom of Hungary that was formally established by the crowning of the Magyar prince István (Stephen) at the beginning of the eleventh century incorporated much of the former Moravian territory, including all of modern-day Slovakia. The Slavic peoples of this territory, the ancestors of the modern Slovaks, were thereby separated politically from those of the western territories, the Czechs, for most of the time between the collapse of Moravia and the formation of Czechoslovakia in 1918. The name Moravia itself came to refer only to a relatively small region that had been located in the west-central part of Svätopluk's domains.

THE RISE AND FALL OF BOHEMIA

During the tenth century, this truncated Moravia came under the control of a rising power to the west, Bohemia, and from that time on the destinies of Bohemia and Moravia have been closely interwined. Under the rule of the Přemyslid Dynasty, Bohemia expanded and defended its territories against Germans to the west, Poles to the north, and Magyars to the east, finally consolidating its domains by the middle of the eleventh century within borders that remained mostly stable for the next three centuries. In 1335, the region known as

Silesia, long disputed by Bohemia and Poland, joined the Bohemian crownlands, although the sixteen small Silesian principalities continued to be ruled by native princes of the Piast Dynasty. The status of Silesia thus became a sensitive issue in the relations between Bohemia and Poland at an early date.

The Kingdom of Bohemia developed in a climate of insecurity, surrounded by potentially hostile neighbors. As a counterweight against this insecurity, Bohemia became dependent on the Holy Roman Empire, and in 1212 Emperor Frederick II clarified the relationship by granting Bohemia an imperial charter. Buoyed by this new stability, the Přemyslid monarchs built Bohemia into a major economic and political power.

These early developments prefigured what would be an enduring pattern in Bohemia's history, namely that of a perpetual encounter with neighboring rulers and peoples. In the course of time, this encounter would increasingly take the form of a confrontation between Czechs and Germans, though it must be emphasized that the nationalistic conflict implied by this did not emerge until the modern era. Indeed, the Přemyslid king Václav I (1230-53) welcomed and encouraged German colonists in his realm, thereby facilitating the close association of two ethnic communities that would clash bitterly 700 years later. In the meantime, however, the Přemyslids—as well as their dynastic successors the Luxemburgs—were justly unconcerned with ethnic questions, for their world of the late Middle Ages had not yet seen the rise of popular nationalism.[2]

Bohemia's wealth and influence grew once again under the rule of the last Přemyslid king, Václav II (1278-1305), and continued during the reign of the Luxemburgs, who first ascended the throne in 1310. Rich silver mines, developed in towns such as Kutná Hora, formed the basis of a booming economy that propelled Bohemia into an era of prosperity and power. Upper and Lower Lusatia were added to the crownlands, enhancing the international prestige of the Bohemian monarchs. The high point of Bohemia's glory was reached during the reign of Charles I of the Luxemburg Dynasty, who was crowned Holy Roman Emperor Charles IV in 1355. Prague became the empire's capital, and Charles saw to it that his city reflected the grandeur of his title. Architects, painters, and sculptors were imported from other lands to create monumental landmarks, a great many of which stand today. Charles founded the first university in central Europe, an institution that still bears his name in socialist Czechoslovakia. By the time of his death in 1378, Charles had established Prague as a major cultural and political center in the heart of Europe, ruling directly over a kingdom stabilized by charters and institutions shaped by the king himself and exercising authority over all the lands of the Holy Roman Empire. The legacy of Charles IV has been deservedly treasured by every subsequent generation of Czechs, many of whom have considered that era to be among the finest·in their nation's checkered history.

The crown of the empire left Prague upon Charles's death and was not brought back until it was worn by the Habsburg ruler Rudolf II at the end of the sixteenth century. In the meantime, the Bohemian kingdom passed through a time of religious and political upheaval, civil war, dynastic conflicts, and the rise of a powerful aristocracy that assumed the prerogative of electing the monarch. This is not to say that Bohemia stagnated during the entire period; some considerable progress was achieved in the arts and letters, particularly under the rule of the mercurial Emperor Rudolf II, whose personal quirks included a fanatical devotion to the fine arts.

Hus and the Hussites

From the early years of the fifteenth century, questions of religion came to dominate the history of the Bohemian kingdom. To set the context in which this developed, let us backtrack briefly. Christianity had become established among the Slavs of this region centuries earlier; most conventional histories trace the origins of Christianity to the building of the first church in Nitra (A.D. 836) and the baptism of fourteen Czech noblemen in Regensburg in 845. There is some evidence that Christianity had first come as much as two centuries before that.[3] The tenth-century ruler Václav (St. Wenceslas), Bohemia's patron saint, was instrumental in spreading Christianity throughout the realm. A bishopric was established in Prague under the rule of Přemysl Boleslav II (c. 973), and in the thirteenth century the right of investiture of bishops was granted to the Bohemian monarch. The Bishropric of Prague was elevated to an arch-bishopric in 1344, during the reign of John of Luxemburg. Then, under the rule of Charles IV, a movement for church reform began, picking up strength during the reign of Václav IV (Charles IV's son and heir to the Bohemian throne). It was at the height of this reform movement that the great religious leader Jan Hus entered the scene.

Hus, the son of a peasant from south Bohemia, became dean of the philosophy faculty at Prague University in 1401, amid a conflict between Czech and foreign elements (primarily German) within the university. In the following year, Hus also began preaching in Prague's Bethlehem Chapel, where it had become the custom to preach sermons in the Czech vernacular rather than the conventional Latin. Hus drew a great deal of inspiration from his fourteenth-century predecessor Jan Milič (d. 1374), who sought to purify the church and bring it closer to the people. Hus also came to be influenced by the writings of the English theologian John Wycliffe, who had attacked the doctrine of transubstantiation and fought for reforms in the organization of the church.

Hus's religious teachings were hotly debated. He was strongly opposed by Archbishop Zbyněk and the foreign masters of the university, who represented a majority of the faculty. For political reasons, however, King Václav supported Hus for the moment; in 1409 the king changed the university statutes to give the Czechs a majority, causing most of the foreign masters to resign and Hus to be elected rector of the university. From this position Hus continued to develop his own theological critique. He publicly condemned the sale of indulgences, argued for the dispensation of both species (bread and wine) in the eucharist, and openly challenged the doctrine of papal infallibility. These activities brought him into conflict with Rome, and in 1414 Hus was summoned to appear before an ecclesiastical council in Constance to justify his position. He had been promised safe conduct to Constance, which lay in the domains of King Sigismund, a half-brother and bitter rival to Václav of Bohemia. In Constance, however, Hus was imprisoned, given a brief hearing, and condemned. Sigismund's promise of safe conduct proved insincere, and on July 6, 1415, Jan Hus was burned at the stake.

The execution of Hus provoked a rebellion in Bohemia, for the reformer had attracted a powerful following among his native noblemen. Hussitism, as the movement now came to be called, spread and became militantly defiant. A crisis developed when Sigismund attempted to claim the Bohemian throne upon the death of Václav in 1419. There ensued a period of protracted conflict, the so-called Hussite Wars. At first the conflict was fought between the Czech Hussites and foreign armies dispatched by neighboring rulers supported by the pope. In time, the Hussites successfully held off their foreign enemies and then started to fight each other. Several sects grew up within the Hussite movement, such as the communal Táborites and the fanatical Adamites. These fratricidal conflicts did not destroy the overall power of the Hussites, however; under the leadership of several brilliant military commanders, including Prokop the Bald and the blind Jan Žižka, the Hussites overcame their differences; established their position firmly; won the right to practice their new religion in Bohemia, Moravia, and Silesia; and even managed to spread their beliefs by means of missionary efforts in Hungarian-ruled Slovakia. Bohemia's religious rights were legitimated by the Compacts of Prague, written up in 1433 and agreed to in 1436 by Sigismund, the enemy king who had in the meantime become Emperor of Rome. Although not accepted by the pope, the Compacts served as the legal foundation of Protestantism in Bohemia for nearly two centuries thereafter.

Hussitism was indeed a form of Protestantism, begun in reformist zeal against the practices of the Roman church a century before the Lutheran Reformation. The Hussites consolidated their theology around the moderate doctrine of Utraquism, justifying the dispensation of both bread and wine to the laity. Their church was headed by an archbishop independent of Rome. By the middle of the fifteenth century, the majority of the nobles had become Protestants, and in 1458 the estates of Bohemia elected the first Protestant king in Europe, Jiří (George) of Poděbrady. King Jiří ruled for only thirteen years, but during that time he made his own contribution to Czech and European history by being the first ruler to propose an international league among monarchs to maintain peace.

Amid these remarkable events, yet another important religious thinker emerged, Petr Chelčický (1390–1460). Chelčický founded a pacifistic group known as the Brethren, among whose contributions was the translation of the Bible into Czech in the sixteenth century. Later, during the Counter-Reformation, most of the Brethren fled their homeland, many of them migrating by way of Moravia and later Saxony; some came to America in the eighteenth century, where they established the Moravian Church.

The Hussites not only brought about the dominance of Protestantism in Bohemia but also reasserted the independence of the Bohemian estates. One might see the events of this era as precocious expressions of a kind of Czech nationalism, for the religious conflict and even the scholarly controversy at Prague University had pitted Czechs against foreigners. Moreover, the theological ferment that culminated in the works of Hus and Chelčický represented a monumental national contribution to European intellectual history; Martin Luther later acknowledged that Hus's teachings had influenced him greatly, and it is therefore no exaggeration to say that the Reformation really began in Bohemia.

The "Darkness"

Upon the death of the Hussite King Jiří in 1471, the Bohemian estates turned to a Polish prince and elected him King Vladislav II. In 1490, he became King of Hungary as well, and from this time on the two kingdoms were drawn into close interaction. When Vladislav's son and heir, Louis, died in 1526, both crowns were left vacant. The Hungarian crown was quickly claimed by the archduke Ferdinand of Austria, and after some maneuvering he managed also to ascend the throne of Bohemia. Ferdinand thus became the first of many subsequent members of the Habsburg family to rule over Bohemia. Ferdinand immediately came into conflict with the estates, and the history of Bohemia during the next hundred years was a chronicle of struggle between the monarch and the nobles. Continuing political and religious divisions among the nobles enabled Ferdinand, with the help of some legal chicanery, to reestablish the principle of hereditary succession. He thereby secured the crown for future generations of Habsburgs despite substantial misgivings in the estates.

These misgivings erupted into a confrontation during the reign of Ferdinand's grandson Rudolf II (1576–1611). By this time the Reformation in Germany had engulfed Europe in a swirling tumult, spilling over into the Habsburg domains and threatening the stability of all the crownlands. Rudolf clumsily attempted to eliminate Protestantism in Hungary and lost the Hungarian crown to the rebel king Matthias. Matthias eventually succeeded in forcing Rudolf's total abdication and in 1611 ascended the imperial throne. Matthias, however, was also a Catholic, and he proved to be no more tolerant of Bohemian Protestantism than his predecessor. A controversy over the rights of Protestants in Bohemia resulted in the so-called Defenestration of Prague (1618), in which two prominent members of the king's governing council were thrown out of a window in Prague Castle. It did not matter that they landed in the moat and escaped with minor injuries, for the defenestration signaled the beginning of a revolt by the Bohemian estates—a revolt that began as a reassertion of the nobles' religious and political rights, led to the temporary overthrow of Habsburg rule in Bohemia, triggered the Thirty Years' War in central Europe, and brought about the tragic destruction of Bohemia as a sovereign state.

The Thirty Years' War was an event of great complexity, escalating into a general European conflagration in which Protestant and Catholic forces fought each other more or less to a draw, finally ending in the Treaty of Westphalia (1648). The treaty settled many long-standing religious and political quarrels that had arisen out of the Reformation by establishing the prerogative of each sovereign to determine the religion of his land. Unfortunately for the Protestants of Bohemia, however, the treaty restored neither their religion nor their independence. Early in the war, Bohemia had succumbed to an invasion by the Habsburg forces and their Catholic allies. The decisive moment had come at the Battle of White Mountain, near Prague, in 1620: Bohemia's army, under the leadership of the recently elected King Frederick of the Palatinate, was defeated and sent scurrying in disarray as Frederick (the "Winter King") fled into exile. Though the general war widened into an all-European conflict, Bohemia's war had ended early in ignominious defeat.

Ferdinand II, the Habsburg ruler who had succeeded Matthias, recaptured Bohemia for the Habsburgs and set about reclaiming the "kingdom of heretics" for Catholicism. Protestant noblemen were exterminated, their properties confiscated and given over to a new nobility called in from Catholic lands to settle in Bohemia. Jesuits were brought in to reconvert the population to Catholicism. In 1627, Ferdinand enacted a new constitution that abolished all the political rights of the Bohemian estates, established Catholicism as the sole religion, certified hereditary succession to the throne, and introduced German as the official language. Nominally, Bohemia (together with Moravia and Silesia) remained a separate kingdom, but in reality it became no more than a province of the sprawling Habsburg domains ruled from Vienna. The flower of Bohemian society went into exile—some 35,000 families, including all the leading cultural and intellectual figures such as the brilliant and world-renowned educator Jan Amos Komenský (Comenius). With the downfall of the Bohemian kingdom, Czech culture went into eclipse and Czech society entered a long period of oppression sometimes referred to as the time of "darkness."

This "darkness" was not entirely unmitigated; some positive development continued. The legacy of the seventeenth and eighteenth centuries includes, for example, a wealth of baroque art and architecture that can be seen throughout the Czech lands today. Although not the work of Czechs, some scholarship took place in the ancient university city. Among other creative personalities of this era, Mozart was attracted to Prague and found in it a congenial atmosphere for a temporary home. In the late eighteenth century, industry began to develop in Bohemia and Moravia as the great landlords turned some of their energies toward manufacturing. Yet the character of the period was nonetheless that of colonialism; an outside power ruled over the land through an aristocracy whose primary loyalty was to the imperial center rather than to the native masses who spoke a separate language and were excluded from power and privilege. There is therefore a great deal of validity to the mythic imagery of "darkness" popularly ascribed to the seventeenth and eighteenth centuries, and, notwithstanding the fact that life continued to go on, it is true that the national identity of the Czechs was nearly lost.

THE NATIONAL AWAKENINGS

The winds of nationalism swept across Europe in the latter part of the eighteenth century and the beginning of the nineteenth. A primordial instinct compelling people to identify with potent symbols of their native culture, as Johann Gottfried Herder and other European spokesmen described it, nationalism proved also to be a political phenomenon, linked to specific events in the development of society and manipulable by men interested in power, social progress, moral rearmament, or the purposeful integration of modern communities. Nationalism therefore did not simply spring up by accident; it arose out of the dynamics of the modern era, propelled in different societies at varying rates of speed and by varying social agents. Forces released by the French Revolution, carried along in France by the bourgeoisie, found their expression in Poland and Hungary mostly among the nobility. Ideas generated by democratic French revolutionaries were manipulated by the demagogue Napoleon to his own advantage and accompanied his army as it crossed Europe. Peoples in the central and eastern regions of the continent were moved by nationalism to challenge the rule of foreigners, just as the middle classes of the west were driven to rebel against their own aristocratic countrymen in the name of the nation.

Czechs and Slovaks were by no means immune to these sentiments, despite the "darkness" that had descended upon the Bohemian crownlands in the seventeenth century and the much longer subjugation of the Slovaks. In the course of the nineteenth century a resurgence of national culture took place among both peoples. The resurgence was remarkable not only because of the politically oppressive conditions in which it took root but also because, unlike other paradigms of central European nationalism, the Czech and Slovak revivals developed without the benefit of native aristocracies.

Paradoxically, it was during the height of Habsburg absolutism that the awakenings began, and even more paradoxically, the national movements that would one day contribute to the disintegration of the monarchy were set in motion by the policies of the absolutist monarchs. Empress Maria Theresa (1740–80) and her son Joseph II (1780–90) succeeded in centralizing their personal power by greatly diminishing that of the church and the nobility. Protestantism was legalized, encouraging some of the national "awakeners" among both Czechs and Slovaks to return to what they considered their native religion. In Bohemia and Moravia, the nobility for a while became interested in the language spoken by the common folk, partly as a curiosity but also partly as a means of reestablishing a lost identity within the centralized empire. Later, this non-Czech nobility would lose interest in Czech culture and even regret the political force that emerged from it, but in the eighteenth century no one could have predicted the eventual ramifications. In 1784 a group of nobles founded what was to become the Royal Bohemian Academy of Science, an organization aimed at promoting the exploration of Czech culture. Seven years later Emperor Leopold II, in a concession to this seemingly harmless curiosity, established a professorship in Czech at Charles University in Prague. These two institutions became the seedbed of a small but influential scholarly community whose efforts at studying and promoting the Czech language were the vital foundation of Czech nationalism.

Similarly in Hungary, which was weakened by the long Turkish occupation, the policies of Habsburg absolutism paved the way for a new interest in the native cultures. It was at this time that the first consciousness of the Slovaks as a separate ethnic group began to evolve. This consciousness was slow to take shape, for the Slovaks lacked their own literary tradition; as of the late eighteenth century, the only written form of their language was that of their Bible, which had come to them via Hussite missionaries and was, therefore, a Czech literary language quite distinct from the Slovak vernacular. Pioneering work in Slovak linguistics was undertaken around the turn of the century by a Roman Catholic priest, Anton Bernolák, and in 1803 an Institute of Slavonic Languages and Literature was founded at the Lutheran lyceum in Pressburg (Bratislava) under the professorship of Juraj Palkovič (1769–1850). Thus in the early years of the nineteenth century the groundwork for a Slovak national movement was laid.

Development of the National Movements

The national awakenings went through three phases of development.[4] The first was characterized by the painstaking scholarly work of philologists who sought to rediscover, codify, and update the native tongues; these included the Slovaks Bernolák and Palkovič and their counterparts among the Czechs, particularly Josef Dobrovský (1773–1829) and Josef Jungmann (1773–1847). Their work was, in a sense, "purely" scholarly: although their studies of the native languages spilled over into work on culture and history, they did not actively seek to politicize their countrymen and indeed had little direct impact on the wider society.

The political implications of their work, however, were quite clearly perceived by the next generation of "awakeners," whose activities initiated the second phase of national development. The circle of intellectuals associated with the awakening widened, the scholarly work deepened and broadened. A new literature emerged, debates about proper linguistic forms took place, and the writing of serious history began. The participants' sense of commitment to their mother tongue grew into a kind of patriotism focused upon the common culture of their own heritage. They considered their national culture a precious birthright and strove to diffuse a consciousness of it among their countrymen. High points in this phase of development were the opening of the Matice česká (Czech Foundation) in 1831 and the appearance of the multivolume *History of the Czech People* written by the outstanding historian František Palacký (1798–1876), the first volume of which was published in 1836. In addition to Palacký, several other important personalities entered the stage during this second phase: the Czech romantic poet Karel Hynek Mácha (1810–36), the Slovak literateur-philologist L'udovít Štúr (1815–56), and two important Slovaks who worked closely with the Czech movement, Jan Kollár (1793–1852), a poet, and the archeologist Pavol Josef Šafárik (1795–1861), who chose to stress his preference for Czech literary forms by adopting the Czech spelling of his name: Pavel Josef Šafařík.

It was during this phase that a very important division occurred within the Slovak national awakening. Kollár and Šafařík, who were attracted by the Pan-Slavic conception of a great brotherhood among all Slavic peoples, believed that Slovaks and Czechs were of the same national stock. Štúr, on the other hand, believed them to be quite distinct. While Kollár and Šafařík worked to draw the two literary movements together, Štúr sought to emphasize the distinctiveness of the Slovak language and culture. His most important contribution was a major codification of the Slovak language in which he chose dialects from central and eastern Slovakia as the basis of his literary language. These dialects were closer to the vernacular of more Slovaks than the western dialect preferred by Kollár and Bernolák before him—but more distant from Czech. Štúr's work therefore served to distinguish Slovak from Czech, and from the 1840s on Slovak literary development took a separate path.

1848. Near the middle of the century, however, the Czech and Slovak movements were momentarily brought together by political developments, as each movement entered its third critical phase. This phase saw the actual spread of national consciousness to a broader spectrum of society and the emergence of overtly political activities associated with nationalism.

The first major event unfolded in 1848, the year of revolutions throughout Europe. A group of Czechs, under the leadership of Palacký and the journalist Karel Havlíček (1820–56), demanded autonomous status for Bohemia within the Austrian Empire. Rejecting an invitation to join with Germans in the revolutionary Frankfurt Parliament, the Czechs instead turned their efforts toward their ethnic cousins of Eastern Europe and convoked a Pan-Slavic Congress. The Congress assembled in Prague on June 2, 1848, and passed a number of resolutions including one that demanded autonomy for all of the historic crownlands within the Habsburg Empire. The decorous deliberations of the Slavic Congress gave way a few days later to demonstrations in the streets, whereupon imperial troops entered Prague and suppressed the revolt.

The demand for a decentralized monarchy was not granted; nevertheless, the short-lived revolt of 1848 was of considerable significance for the further development of the nationalist movements. It was the first political expression of a Czech national identity in the modern era, drawing the support of some workers as well as a part of the middle class; their numbers were not great, but their courageous stand inspired many of their countrymen and encouraged further actions on behalf of the national cause. Importantly, the events of 1848 were felt in Slovakia, too, as restless intellectuals raised political demands on behalf of the Slovak nation. Some Slovaks were brought temporarily into cooperation with the Czechs. Štúr, for example, was one of several who journeyed from Slovakia to Prague for the Pan-Slavic Conference. Although Czech-Slovak collaboration was interrupted soon thereafter, a precedent was set for the movement that would eventually lead to political unification and independence.

After 1848. For more than a decade following the revolt of 1848, the new Austrian monarch Franz Joseph ruled over the restless national groups with an iron hand. Then, however, a renewed crisis within the empire led to war with Piedmont and France, resulting in the loss of Italy. The weakened monarchy in Vienna now sought to stabilize its relationship with the Hungarians, whose revolt in 1848–49 had nearly succeeded in overthrowing Austrian rule. At first it appeared that concessions would be made to Bohemia as well, but in the end the emperor decided on autonomy for Hungary only; the historic Compromise of 1867 established the Dual (Austro-Hungarian) Monarchy, placating the Hungarians but not the other nationalities. Czech nationalists tried again and again to raise the question of Bohemia, but they were unsuccessful. A glimmer of hope appeared in 1871, when Prime Minister Karl Hohenwart proposed a program of autonomy for the Bohemian crownlands. In the end, however, the emperor rejected the Hohenwart program because of strong opposition among the Hungarians as well as the Germans in the Vienna parliament. This effectively sounded the death knell of the conservative Czech program, based on claims to the ancient rights of the crownlands, and opened the door for the gradual emergence of newer forces representing a more modern, democratic nationalism.

From this time until the turn of the century, Czechs and Slovaks went their separate ways. The Compromise of 1867 had given the Hungarians exclusive rule over the territories inhabited by Slovaks, while the Bohemian crownlands (minus the larger part of Silesia, which had fallen under Prussian rule in the eighteenth century) were ruled by Vienna. The two ruling systems that developed in the separate halves of the empire were very different. In Austria, the political situation evolved gradually and ineluctably in a democratic direction as the aristocracy slowly yielded increasing degrees of power to a broader portion of society, culminating in the introduction of universal male suffrage in 1906. In Hungary, on the contrary, the political franchise broadened very little in practice as the traditional aristocracy clung to its favored position; franchise laws restricted voting rights to propertied citizens, and elections, which were not held by means of secret ballot but instead were closely scrutinized by officials, were marred by frequent corruption and occasional brutality. Therefore, as more and more Czechs entered Austrian politics at all levels, only a handful of Slovaks attained any positions of political importance before World War I.

In the Bohemian crownlands, a lively and pluralistic political life developed toward the end of the nineteenth century. Earlier, the so-called Old Czech Party of Palacký and his son-in-law František Rieger had lost its dominance in Czech politics to the Young Czech Party. The Young Czechs had formed their party in the 1870s and gradually attracted the support of farmers, shopkeepers, and artisans who preferred their liberal approach to the nationalist program over the more conservative programs of the Old Czechs. Meanwhile, the economic development that had begun in the eighteenth century intensified and created an industrial boom that catapulted Bohemia and Moravia into the front ranks of the Habsburg-ruled lands. Along with industrialization came an increasingly differentiated social structure, and this in turn gave impetus to further new political groupings. By 1910 there were an active Social Democratic Party, a Catholic party, and an agrarian party among the Czechs, in addition to some smaller groups such as Masaryk's Realist Party. All of these competed effectively against German parties operating in Bohemia and Moravia, giving the Czechs strong national representation not only in local and provincial governments but also in the imperial parliament.

In Slovakia, political life underwent a much more limited development up to the time of the First World War. This was largely due to the more restrictive nature of the Hungarian political system, but in part it was attributable to the low level of socioeconomic development. Generally speaking, Slovakia's pattern of economic development was not unlike that of Hungary. Industrial centers were growing in the lowlands, especially in places where large numbers of ethnic Hungarians lived, for example Pozsony (Bratislava), Kassa (Košice), and in the valleys of the lower Váh and Hron rivers, but the hinterlands were undeveloped and largely out of touch with the modern world. By the turn of the century a few factories had sprung up in the interior regions, notably around Rózsahegy (Ružomberok) in Liptó County. These were very significant from the political point of view, because they represented the growth of industrialization in regions where the overwhelming majority of the population were Slovaks. Thus there developed the basis for a smallish urban proletariat and, much more importantly, a wealthy bourgeoisie capable of supporting a Slovak political movement.

This Slovak movement faced great obstacles. Not only did the franchise laws militate against the Slovaks' political prospects, but from 1875 on the Hungarian government pursued forcible assimilationist policies toward the non-Magyar communities by means of increasingly coercive methods. The Matica slovenská, an institution founded in 1863 along the lines of the Czech Matice, was closed, as were Slovak-language secondary schools. Slovaks who were unwilling to assimilate met discrimination in education, business, and government service, and Slovak political activists were persecuted. Given the pressures to assimilate into Hungarian culture and the hazards of opposition activities, it is amazing that a Slovak political movement was able to grow and flourish during the two decades prior to 1914. It is even more remarkable that this took place during a period when some 20 percent or more of the population left Slovakia and emigrated to other lands, although it must be said that the nationalist movement received a great deal of much-needed support, both moral and financial, from émigrés abroad, especially in America.

THE CZECHOSLOVAK IDEA
AND THE INDEPENDENCE MOVEMENT

Under these circumstances the idea of a "Czechoslovak" nation took hold among the most important leaders of both movements. The notion that Czechs and Slovaks shared a common cultural heritage can be traced back at least to Kollár, but the idea had temporarily lost its salience in the subsequent unfolding of events. The linguistic work of Štúr had encouraged and solidified the separateness of the two literary cultures, and the Compromise of 1867 had erected a seemingly impenetrable political barrier between the two nations. In the 1890s, however, increased contacts between Czechs and Slovaks reestablished a strong community of interest. A number of important Czech intellectuals began to take an interest in the Slovaks; among them was Tomáš Masaryk, then a professor at Prague University and himself half Slovak. In 1896 some of Masaryk's students formed the Czechoslovak Union, and in 1898 the first issue of the journal *Hlas* (The Voice) was published in the Slovak town of Skalica by two of the union's members, Vavro Šrobár and Pavol Blaho. *Hlas* quickly became the mouthpiece of a young and energetic group of political activists whose increasingly radical position openly challenged the leaders of the old National Party.

The National Party had arisen in the 1860s. Headquartered in the sleepy mountain town of Turčiansky Svätý Martin, it was hardly a political party in the conventional sense but rather an organization of intellectuals who published a newspaper, *Národnie noviny* (National News), and sought to advance Slovak educational and political rights by whatever means available within the restricted context of the Hungarian system. In the decade 1900–10 the party did nominate candidates for election to the Hungarian parliament, but its organization remained rather loose and unstructured in comparison to the modern political parties of Bohemia. Traditionally Pan-Slavic in their orientation, the older leaders of the National Party were skeptical of the radical ideas circulating in *Hlas*, but in the course of time many of the party's leaders came over to the Czechoslovak side.

Two more Slovak groups came together during these years. The Slovak People's Party was founded in 1905 by a fiery young priest, Andrej Hlinka. At about the same time, Milan Hodža, a young Lutheran editing a Slovak newspaper in Budapest, stepped into the political spotlight. These two men were destined to play leading roles in Slovakia's politics for the next thirty years. At this early point they shared the objective of organizing the Slovak peasantry into a political force, although after 1918 they would find that their ideological positions were poles apart and their interpretations of Slovakia's best interests in conflict. From 1905 to the end of World War I, however, they found themselves fighting for the same cause—Slovak political rights.

Although the Czech and Slovak nationalist movements now drew closer together, neither was self-consciously an independence movement prior to the outbreak of the war, and in fact the ultimate ends of Czechoslovak cooperation were by no means clear even to Masaryk and Šrobár. It was only during the war that they changed their fundamental orientation from autonomy to independence.

The outbreak of World War I caught Czechs and Slovaks in an uncomfortable situation. For some of them Pan-Slavic sympathies were still warm, and being obliged to fight against fellow Slavs (Serbs and Russians) was an unpleasant turn of events. Equally unpleasant was the necessity to fight and die for a foreign monarch (Franz Joseph), who in his doddering old age had become the butt of many jokes among the iconoclastic Czechs. Large numbers of Czech and Slovak troops defected to the Russian side, and a sizable troop contingent known as the Czechoslovak Legion formed in Russia to cooperate with the enemy of the Austro-Hungarian Empire. Back home, the hardships of war and the tightening of the emperor's police surveillance turned many Czechs and Slovaks against the monarchy. In these circumstances the arguments for independence and for Czechoslovak unity in opposition to the monarchy became very persuasive.

Masaryk became the clear leader of the independence movement. In exile throughout the war, he traveled widely, seeking support among the Allied powers but also maintaining contact with the underground organization known as the "Mafia" back home. Together with his younger colleague Edvard Beneš, Masaryk worked tirelessly to persuade the Western leaders that the Czechoslovak idea was viable. Masaryk and Beneš were joined in this diplomatic effort by Milan R. Štefánik, a Slovak astronomer who had become a French citizen and fought in the French Air Corps. The exiled leaders formed a Czechoslovak Foreign Committee in November 1915, which was superseded by the Czechoslovak National Council in 1916. The council's cause was aided by the support of Czech- and Slovak-Americans, although the latter were by no means united in their enthusiasm for the Czechoslovak idea. In fact, the reservations felt by many Slovak-Americans were expressed quite clearly throughout Masaryk's discussions with them, and when their leaders finally signed an agreement with Masaryk in May 1918 pledging their support for an independent Czechoslovak state, they insisted on a clause promising autonomy for Slovakia. This Pittsburgh Declaration of 1918 later became the cause of great controversy among Slovaks and Czechs; however, for the time being it gave Masaryk additional ammunition in his quest for Allied support. Not long thereafter, he persuaded President Woodrow Wilson to support the independence movement, and the goal of an independent Czechoslovakia became Allied policy.

In the meantime, the Austro-Hungarian Empire had begun to come apart at the seams. Weakened by war and threatened by nationalist movements within, the monarchy grew more and more shaky. Franz Joseph died in 1916 after sixty-eight years of rule. His successor, Karl (Charles), unsuccessfully explored the possibilities of a separate peace with the enemy in order to save his empire. Yet even before the end of the war, the empire disintegrated. The Czech and Slovak leaders, realizing that the monarchy was no longer able to hold itself together, made plans for a declaration of independence. With Wilson's approval, a Czechoslovak provisional government was organized; on October 28, 1918, this group met with representatives of the Czechoslovak National Committee who had journeyed from Prague to Geneva, and independence was proclaimed. A similar proclamation was issued in Prague and, two days later, in Turčiansky Svätý Martin. What had seemed impossible and indeed unrealistic four years earlier had become a reality: the birth of an independent Czechoslovakia.

INDEPENDENT CZECHOSLOVAKIA: THE FIRST REPUBLIC

Surveys of public opinion taken in 1946 and again in 1968 revealed a strong tendency among Czechs to view the First Czechoslovak Republic (1918–38) as the greatest moment of their national history.[5] Without passing judgment on that collective perception, it should be added that the view is not so widely shared by Slovaks. Nonetheless, it is indisputable that the First Republic was a grand and noble political achievement, and whatever its shortcomings it stood for twenty years as a model of constitutional democracy in the midst of a Europe teetering on the brink of its own destruction. Alone among the new states of the post-World War I order and alone in Central Europe, the Czechoslovak republic withstood the many threats to its existence from within—from unassimilated nationalities, extremist ideologies, and the economic ravages of the depression—and succumbed only when these internal enemies were aided by the crushing force of a foreign aggressor too powerful to be resisted.

From the time of its creation, the Czechoslovak state was critically dependent for its survival on a hospitable international environment. One can speculate whether or not independence could have been achieved without Allied support, but it is indisputable that the statesmen who drew up the Peace of Paris in 1919 could easily have condemned Czechoslovakia to oblivion by their disapproval. Nor was the certainty of Czechoslovakia's survival guaranteed by the Paris treaties; hostile neighbors surrounded the small republic, and although most of them were individually weak, together they posed a serious threat. Therefore, Czechoslovakia's leaders found it expedient to enter into alliances with friendly outside forces. Treaties with Yugoslavia and Romania (1920–21) formed the basis of what came to be called the Little Entente among these three states, all of which were threatened by Hungarian claims on their territories. In 1924 Czechoslovakia signed a mutual defense treaty with France, obviously meant as protection against a resurgent Germany. And, in 1935, a treaty was signed with the Soviet Union, providing for Soviet assistance in the defense of Czechoslovakia but contingent upon France's honoring its commitment to come to Czechoslovakia's aid. This vital network of treaties was created through the skillful diplomacy of the republic's first foreign minister, Edvard Beneš. Unfortunately, the network proved to be brittle. The disaster that befell Czechoslovakia when the French defaulted on their commitment in 1938 tragically illustrated the dependency of the little republic on outside support.

Internally, the founders of the Czechoslovak republic developed a highly creative political order. The framers of the new system drew upon an already substantial political tradition, especially among the Czechs, as they created their governing mechanisms. The First Republic was a unitary state built upon a liberal, Western-style constitution. The system embodied many liberal principles such as separation of church and state, guarantees of individual rights, and due process of law. A bicameral parliament was elected by universal suffrage; the parliament in turn elected the president, who appointed the prime minister and cabinet. Members of parliament were chosen by a complicated method of proportional representation that guaranteed seats to all parties with a substantial electoral constituency.

This factor encouraged the formation of multiple political parties. A number of parties that had formed before 1914 continued to operate in the new republic and were drawn into competition with new parties. Party lines formed around extended interest groups drawn together by common ethnic identity, religion, social class, or some combination of these factors. There were, for example, four socialist parties, including the Communists and the German Social Democrats; two ultrana- tionalist Slovak parties, one of them Catholic and one Protes- tant; a Small Traders' Party as well as another party, the National Democrats, that tended to represent the interests of big business; and various parties representing the smaller ethnic minorities. Over the course of the First Republic's existence, the strongest party proved to be the Republican Party of Farmers and Peasants (commonly called the Agrarian Party). The Agrarians' appeal cut across ethnic lines, drawing support from Czechs and Slovaks alike; led by the Czech Antonín Švehla until his death in 1929, it was also the party of Milan Hodža and had a substan- tial following among the Slovak bourgeoisie. Despite their attractiveness to both rural and urban social groups among the two dominant nationalities, however, the Agrarians' plurality in parliamentary elections never exceeded 15 percent.

This fact tells a great deal about the governments of the First Republic. No single party ever ruled; the closest that one ever came to a majority was in the 1920 elections, when the Czechoslovak Social Democratic Party received slightly more than 25 percent of the vote. (The following year, the left wing of the Social Democrats broke away to form the Communist Party, and the Social Democrats never again gained the leader- ship.) Thus the republic was ruled by a succession of coalition governments made up of four to eight different parties. The governments were generally formed around a center-right or center-left coalition and always included the Agrarians. When these coalitions would come apart, they were sometimes replaced temporarily by a nonpartisan government that would function until a new coalition could be put together.

Masaryk and Beneš

To a considerable extent, the political system was held to- gether by the republic's first president, Masaryk, and his succes- sor, Beneš. Masaryk was a legendary figure whose leadership of the independence movement had given him a national stature reminiscent of George Washington. A man with a towering intellect and great human sensitivity, he has often been referred to as the modern incarnation of Plato's philosopher-king. That may be an exaggeration, but there is no question that Masaryk was widely respected and indeed loved among his countrymen, both Czech and Slovak. Already sixty-nine years old when he became president, Masaryk stood as a father figure during the sixteen years of his presidency. He gathered around himself in the Prague Castle a circle of highly capable men, and together with them he worked out solutions to the seemingly irresolvable problems attending the complex political structure. Until his retirement in 1935 Masaryk played a critical role in the workings of the republic, and it can be accurately said that he, more than anyone else, created and symbolized the First Republic.

His successor, Edvard Beneš, was also a very gifted man. His foreign policy, as already noted, had been successful during the first decade and a half of the republic's existence. It was Beneš's misfortune to become president just at the beginning of the international crisis that developed into World War II, destroying the Czechoslovak republic in its wake. Given the circumstances, it is doubtful that anyone in Beneš's position could have saved Czechoslovakia—including Masaryk, who died in 1937. Certainly Beneš, a man of great courage and political wisdom, tried. His considerable skills were not enough to save his country from Hitler's Germany, nor even to maintain civic unity at the republic's moment of crisis.

Domestic Conflicts

Under the constitution of the First Republic, no corporate rights or privileges were granted to ethnic or national groups. Although this was consistent with the liberal guarantees of individual rights, it caused serious problems as the state system came to be persistently challenged by secessionist and autonomist movements.

The First Republic was dominated by the Czechs, rulers once again in their own country after 300 years of foreign oppression. Still, Czechoslovakia between the wars was an ethnic crazy-quilt in which the Czechs were a plurality but not a majority. Slovaks and Germans each constituted nearly one-fourth of the population; Hungarians between 3 and 5 percent; and Poles, Ukrainians, Jews, and Gypsies still smaller propor-

tions. The Czechs were relatively tolerant (if not entirely under-
standing) of these other communities, but it was clear that the
state embodied values derived more from the Czech political
culture than from any other.

The exact nature of Czechoslovak unity itself became a
bone of contention as Slovak politicians disagreed with each
other about the proper relationship between themselves and the
Czechs. A strong Slovak nationalist movement developed under
the leadership of Father Hlinka. Centered in the Slovak People's
Party, this group sought to amend the constitution to provide
for autonomous political institutions in Slovakia. Basing their
argument on the Pittsburgh Declaration of 1918, the Slovak
nationalists fought doggedly during the 1920s through their
parliamentary representatives, but to no avail. They were
opposed not only by the Czechs but also by a powerful contingent of their fellow Slovaks, led by Hodža and others, who believed that autonomy for the more backward eastern province
would be economically counterproductive and politically dis-
ruptive. The two sides coexisted until Hlinka's death in 1938,
after which more extreme tendencies in the Slovak People's
Party came to the fore. Hlinka's successor, Father Jozef Tiso,
led the party into collusion with Hitler's Germany and thereby
contributed to the demise of the First Republic.

An even more serious challenge came from within the
German minority. The so-called Sudeten Germans had at first
been hostile to the Czechoslovak state in which they found
themselves living after 1918. During the 1920s, however, many
of them came to accept the new republic, and several leading
German politicians served in coalition governments between
1926 and 1938. Just as the Sudeten German problem seemed
to be on the verge of a solution, Adolf Hitler rose to power in
Germany and began to exploit ultranationalistic impulses
among Germans both within Germany's borders and beyond
them. In Czechoslovakia, pro-Hitler elements among the Sudeten
Germans founded the Sudeten German Homeland Front in
1933, renamed the Sudeten German Party two years later. The
new party experienced a phenomenal rise, attracting nearly
two-thirds of the German vote in the 1935 parliamentary elections. Thereafter the party, under the leadership of Konrad

Henlein, drifted more and more into a position of hostile opposition, becoming a fifth column within the Czechoslovak Republic. Although agitating ostensibly for minority rights, Henlein's ultimate objective was to separate the Sudetenland—a rather ill-defined, crescent-shaped territory around the edges of Bohemia and Moravia—from Czechoslovakia and oversee its incorporation into Germany. With Hitler's help, this was accomplished in 1938.

The First Republic in Retrospect

The First Czechoslovak Republic has been the subject of wildly conflicting historical judgments—idealized by its staunchest defenders and condemned by its most vehement critics. It must be admitted that there were flaws in the political system, social and economic inequities, and unresolved problems among the national communities. The wide gap between the more developed Czech economy and the peasant-based Slovak economy did not diminish, and there were extremes of wealth and poverty that tended to be intensified by the Great Depression. Although the working class as a whole was relatively at peace with the political order, there were strikes and demonstrations from time to time; these were sometimes put down with violence, and rebellious leaders were often harassed. As for the nationalities, they too could find cause for dissatisfaction with a state system dominated by Czechs and "Czechoslovaks" who sometimes lacked sensitivity for the burning nationalist feelings of others.

Yet the positive achievements of the First Republic should not be underestimated. For twenty years Czechoslovakia had remained a viable and true democracy, despite being surrounded by increasingly undemocratic and hostile states. Its economy, despite weak spots, was one of the strongest and most advanced in Europe. Whatever their just grievances, Czechoslovakia's minorities were treated with less ethnic discrimination than those of its neighbors—and, to the credit of the dominant Czechs, the other nationalities were better off than the Czechs had been under Austrian rule. This unique interwar experiment with multinational democracy came to an end following the Munich Agreement. Czechs and Slovaks entered yet another time of troubles.

1938–48: CZECHOSLOVAKIA'S CRUCIAL DECADE

To many Czechs, it must have seemed that the events of 1938–45 were an encapsulated repetition of their nation's earlier history, from the White Mountain to the awakening. The period from Munich to the end of World War II was a time of unmitigated national oppression; the German occupation, brutal and humiliating, was all the more disheartening because it shattered the twenty-year euphoria of independence. For Slovaks, the war years were more mixed. Politically separated from the Czech lands, wartime Slovakia was ruled by a native government under Hitler's protection. The Slovak people were deeply divided, however, and emerged from the war badly scarred by the military and political conflict that took place in their country. Reunited at the war's end, Czechs and Slovaks set about piecing together the social and spiritual debris left by the preceding seven years, only to be plunged into another crisis.

Munich, the Second Republic, and the Return of the Darkness

By early 1938 it was clear that Hitler had aggressive designs on Czechoslovakia. In March, he had absorbed Austria, thereby solidifying the German position around the borders of Bohemia and Moravia and adding to his control a common border with Slovakia. For some time he had been encouraging Henlein to make extreme demands on the Prague government for Sudeten autonomy. Czechoslovak Prime Minister Hodža had been negotiating with Henlein for over a year, and Prague had agreed to concessions on minor issues such as the proportion of Germans in government jobs. The scope of Henlein's demands increased, however, and he began to make an international issue out of Prague's alleged insensitivity to its minorities.

Using this as his justification, Hitler himself moved directly into the picture in the late summer of 1938, publicly denouncing Beneš and making dire threats against Czechoslovakia. Hitler appeared quite ready to go to war, if necessary, in order to sever the Sudetenland from Czechoslovakia, but he hoped to avoid war for the moment by neutralizing the French and the British. Beneš, on the other hand, counted on French protection as called for in the 1924 Franco-Czechoslovak treaty, which would in turn activate Prague's 1935 treaty with the Soviet Union. The French government, however, made it clear that it would not act unless it had the backing of the British. Great Britain's Prime Minister Neville Chamberlain, the apostle of appeasement, refused to intervene in defense of Czechoslovakia, and the fate of the latter was thereby sealed.

The government of Czechoslovakia was not represented at the talks held at the end of September in Munich. Present instead were Hitler, Chamberlain, French Prime Minister Edouard Daladier, and Italy's dictator Benito Mussolini. The outcome of the talks was preordained; Chamberlain and Daladier, who had done nothing to stop Hitler's earlier expansionary moves, again acquiesced to the German demands. In a crushing communiqué, Czechoslovak representatives who had been obliged to wait outside the conference chambers were informed that their Western "friends" would not support them if they resisted German annexation of the Sudetenland. With France out of the picture, Beneš could not expect support from the USSR. Alone with his army (well trained and well equipped, but no match for the superior German forces) Beneš decided he had no sensible choice other than capitulation. On October 1, 1938, German troops entered the Sudetenland and met no resistance.

The Munich Agreement has come to symbolize the folly of great-power appeasement in the face of an aggressor whose objectives are unlimited. Whether the French and British really believed they could pacify Hitler so easily or whether they believed they were buying time in order to be better prepared in case war was unavoidable, their capitulation at Munich encouraged Hitler to press further. At the same time, their actions demonstrated an utter lack of moral courage and a callous disregard for a solemn treaty, for the ideals of the League of Nations, and for their own fundamental political values, as they abandoned a democratic ally to a tyrannical foe. The Czechs, who had long prided themselves on their political kinship with the West, learned in 1938 that the West considered them dispensable—a lesson that was subsequently confirmed in 1948 and again in 1968.

Czechoslovakia's other neighbors were quick to take

advantage of the situation, laying hold of territories disputed since 1919. Poland seized Těšín (Cieszyn), and Hungary took a strip of land in southern Slovakia and the eastern region known as Subcarpathian Ruthenia. In Prague, the government tried to persevere in spite of the circumstances. Hodža had been replaced as prime minister in September by General Jan Syrový, the head of a nonpartisan government; Syrový, in turn, was followed in December by Rudolf Beran, an Agrarian who had earlier called for cooperation with Germany. Under pressure from Hitler, Beneš resigned the presidency in October and was replaced by Emil Hácha. Beneš left his country and began anew the long process of political and diplomatic building-in-exile. Back home, the government was further weakened by intensified pressures on the part of the Slovak nationalists and soon agreed to radical constitutional changes. Wide powers of autonomy were granted to Slovakia, which quickly came under the control of the increasingly right-wing Slovak People's Party. The country was officially renamed "Czecho-Slovakia," the hyphenation serving to emphasize a kind of confederative association between the two major parts of the truncated state, and the resulting political system was known as the Second Republic.

The Second Republic was doomed to a very short existence, despite the government's desperate swing to the right and its attempts to placate Hitler. Within six months Hitler demonstrated that his objectives went well beyond the Sudetenland. With his backing, Slovakia seceded on March 14, 1939, and became a separate state allied with Germany. The next day, German troops occupied Bohemia and Moravia, setting up a protectorate over the Czech lands. Although world war was not to break out for another six months, these events ushered in the wartime order for Czechs and Slovaks. In the Protectorate of Bohemia and Moravia, legitimate political parties ceased to exist as German authorities ruled with the collaboration of a hand-picked "Committee of National Trusteeship." Meanwhile, the Slovak state, nominally independent under the clerical-fascist rule of Jozef Tiso, was in reality a satellite of Nazi Germany. The darkness that settled over the lands was indeed painfully reminiscent of that earlier darkness that had been dispelled only twenty years before.

The Road Back to Independence

As German control over the protectorate tightened, resistance activities sprang up among the Czechs. These, however, were relatively limited in their extent and effectiveness. The most notable accomplishment of the resistance was the assassination in 1942 of the top German authority, Reichsprotektor Reinhard Heydrich, by two Czech exiles flown into Bohemia from England. This daring and spectacular event was mostly counterproductive. Although the nation's spirit may have been lifted by the news of Heydrich's death, the Germans retaliated by unleashing a wave of terror that ultimately broke the resistance. Amid the terror, the Bohemian village of Lidice was ruthlessly and totally exterminated; all the men of the village were killed, as were most of the children, while all the women were sent to the Ravensbrück concentration camp. Lidice became a name associated around the world with the atrocities of war. In the occupied Czech lands, the massacre had exactly the intended effect—mass horror, along with the shocking realization that the occupying forces were bound by no laws of human decency. To resist such a force appeared suicidal.

In the Czech lands, therefore, the resistance faded quickly during the second half of the war. The situation was the reverse in Slovakia, where the Tiso regime quite undeniably had substantial popular support in its early years. No doubt there was at least a passive opposition from the very start, but it did not manifest itself actively until later on. When it did, it developed into quite a tenacious force that culminated in the Slovak National Uprising of 1944, a heroic but premature attempt to liberate Slovakia. In many localities, rebel forces found widespread support and cooperation among the civilian population. By the war's end, the Slovaks were bitterly divided between the supporters of the resistance and the remaining adherents of the Tiso regime.

As during the First World War, the most important planning for the country's future took place outside Czechoslovakia. Although a large number of important political leaders suffered imprisonment at the hands of the Nazis, many others escaped into exile. Former President Beneš assembled a government-in-exile based in London. This group of men worked through diplomatic channels to keep the idea of Czechoslovak independence alive. They also maintained contacts with the resistance movements back home, though the severity of political controls there made those connections very tenuous.

During the war the role of the Communists suddenly became important. In the First Republic, the Communists had been one of the five or six most popular parties, but they had always functioned as an opposition and never participated in a governmental coalition. Their ideological backgrounds were mixed; formed in 1921 as the result of a split in the Social Democratic Party, their roots went back into the moderate-left heritage of the pre–World War I social democracy, but the more radical influence of the Soviet-led Communist International (Comintern) became very strong during the 1920s. The influence of the Comintern increased following the election of Klement Gottwald as Party leader in 1929. In the last years before Munich, the Party had turned to a conciliatory stance vis à vis the government, and immediately after Munich the Communists had roundly and publicly denounced the agreement. During the war, the Communists were persecuted and many were imprisoned. Some of the Party's leaders managed to escape into exile; the most important of them, including Gottwald, spent the war years in Moscow, where they were able to consult with Soviet chief Josef Stalin about political strategy. It was at this time that they began to consider the possibility of gaining power in a resurrected Czechoslovakia by working peacefully within a coalition.

Beneš believed it was essential to gain Soviet support in the building of the postwar order, and to this end he personally traveled to Moscow in December 1943. There he concluded a new treaty of alliance with Stalin, signifying the importance of Czechoslovak-Soviet cooperation in Beneš's thinking. While in Moscow, Beneš also spoke with Gottwald and other exiled Czechoslovak Communists and thereby laid the groundwork for cooperation with them. Beneš now began to piece together his plan: Czechoslovakia would be a bridge between East and West, its international position guaranteed by the alliances with both the socialist and the capitalist world, and its domestic politics a blend of liberal democracy with moderate social revolution.

Earlier, President Franklin D. Roosevelt had assured him of America's support; now, with Soviet backing as well, he proceeded to work toward the construction of a new Czechoslovakia.

Cooperation with the Communists was complicated by two factors. In the first place, as Beneš knew, Gottwald was a shrewd politician whose commitment to revolutionary socialism made it difficult for him to accept more moderate approaches to social change. In the second place, the Communists themselves were not entirely united in their vision of the future order, and no version of their ideas coincided with Beneš's—though the latter fact did not become clear immediately at the end of the war.

The Slovak Communists had regrouped as a separate party in the early months of the war, and some of them (including Gustáv Husák) showed some interest in attaching Slovakia to the USSR as a Slovak Soviet Republic. Gottwald, on the other hand, firmly backed the revival of the Czechoslovak state, but one that would be closely allied with the Soviet Union—and, he hoped, ultimately ruled by Communists. His position had the approval of Stalin and eventually won out. By the end of the war it appeared that the Communists were in agreement among themselves concerning their role in a reconstituted Czechoslovakia.

Toward the Communist Victory

Once again, skillful diplomacy had kept Czechoslovakia's cause alive and well in the camp of the victorious powers. In the spring of 1945, Soviet troops broke through German defenses and swept across the country as liberators. In the west, U.S. forces under the command of General George Patton entered and drew to within sixty miles of Prague. The Americans went no further, however. As Prague rose against the Germans in a well-timed uprising (May 5, 1945), it was the Soviet army— not the American—that was given the glorious task of completing the liberation by moving into Prague. This took place quite according to previously agreed-upon Allied plans, but the political implication was clear: among the Allied powers, the Soviet Union had the greater interest in Czechoslovakia and would play the greater role in its postwar development.

Czechoslovakia was reunited, though the territory of Sub-carpathian Ruthenia had been ceded to the Soviet Union before the end of the war. The exiled leaders returned and were joined by those who had survived the concentration camps. Their task of reconstructing the political, economic, and social order was complicated by the bitter divisions the war had created. It was decided to expel the Sudeten Germans, except for those who could demonstrate that they had been antifascist. This was carried out, effectively bringing an end to the 700-year coexistence of Czechs and Germans that had turned into such an ugly twentieth-century conflict.

According to an agreement reached among the country's leaders in newly liberated Košice (April 1945), the government's program promised to outlaw fascist organizations and punish traitors and collaborators. Former parties of the Right were also outlawed on the grounds that some of their members had been guilty of cooperating with the Germans. This provision banned not only the Fascist Party and the Slovak People's Party, whose memberships were thoroughly tainted by collaboration, but also others such as the Agrarians of whom only some members had been truly guilty. The elimination of the former right-wing parties stacked the new political order in favor of the Left, and indeed the parties that were allowed to regroup were brought together loosely within the framework of the National Front. Thus, in the technical sense, there were no opposition parties in the new order. The political system that emerged and lasted until February 1948 was called the Third Republic.

The Košice program had also spelled out the role of the so-called national committees called into being to organize administration on the local level. Beneš, in his earlier discussions with the Communists, had had some misgivings about these vaguely defined institutions, and in reality they turned out to be effective vehicles for the Communists to use in spreading their influence. The national committees were active in identifying and discrediting alleged traitors in many localities, and they contributed as well to the Communists' campaign efforts in the 1946 elections. In that year, the Communists attracted a plurality of the vote: 40.17 percent of the total votes cast, entitling them to 114 seats in the National Assembly. It is generally agreed that the 1946 elections were conducted fairly and honestly—allowing for the fact that voters could be disqualified by unsubstantiated accusations of wartime collaboration. In any event, the Communist vote was gained through neither fraud nor intimidation and reflected a genuine leftward drift of popular sentiment.

Edvard Beneš had assumed the position of acting president upon his return from exile, and he retained that position until 1948. Jan Masaryk, son of the first president, was foreign minister. Klement Gottwald, the Communist leader, had been named interim prime minister in 1945, and the 1946 elections confirmed him in that role. In his cabinet, Communists held several strategically important portfolios, notably the ministries of agriculture, information, internal trade, finance, and the interior (including responsibility for the police and civil administration). From these vantage points the Communists were able to manipulate a wide range of politically important functions, creating a solid base of social control that facilitated their rise to total power.

The power takeover occurred in February 1948, a date that the Communists have celebrated ever since as "victorious February." There was no revolutionary seizure of power by the workers, nor in fact was there any overt violence accompanying what one observer has called the "elegant coup."[6] In a sense, the Communists were ushered into total power by their non-Communist partners in the coalition government. A crisis had been building within the National Front for nearly a year as the Communists blatantly used the internal security forces to discredit opponents and advance their own political aims. A confrontation developed within the cabinet, and on February 20, twelve non-Communist ministers resigned; they apparently hoped that President Beneš would dissolve the government and form a new one that would reorganize the Interior Ministry and the police.

Beneš vacillated, however, and communications between him and the non-Communist ministers broke down. Gottwald, as prime minister, quickly declared a state of emergency, mobilizing the militia in and around Prague. Trade unions, by this time mostly under Communist control, staged a one-hour general strike. Non-Communist politicians were harassed and their offices closed down. Amid this impressive show of force, Gottwald presented Beneš with a list of candidates for a new cabinet clearly weighted in the Communists' favor. Beneš, now an old and sickly man who had been through what seemed a similar situation in 1938, could resist no longer. On February 25, he bowed to Gottwald's pressure and approved the new cabinet.

Gottwald's victory-by-intimidation in February proved to be only a prelude to the Communists' further moves. In the ensuing months they proceeded to eliminate all political opposition and consolidate their hold over social organizations. Their success was punctuated by the deaths of their two most prominent political adversaries. In March, Jan Masaryk died in a fall from a window of his office in the Foreign Ministry; officially his death was attributed to suicide, but evidence disclosed twenty years later supported earlier suspicions that he may have been murdered. Edvard Beneš died in September, three months after resigning from what had become a powerless presidency. There was no mistaking that a new era had begun.

SUMMARY

Czechs and Slovaks have rather separate histories, although in each case their history is intertwined with that of close neighbors. The histories of the Czechs and Slovaks themselves have also become intertwined at a number of important points: during the Hussite era, in the course of the national awakenings, and throughout the independence movement as well as in the independent Czechoslovak Republic. Between 1939 and 1945, Slovakia was separated from the Czech lands; the exiled leaders nevertheless operated under the assumption that the separation was only temporary. Through their efforts the partitioned country was reunified, and the postwar histories of Czechs and Slovaks have once again unfolded together. One should not forget, however, that the two peoples—officially recognized in today's Czechoslovakia as two distinct *nations*—have been politically united for only a relatively short time in their long histories.

Despite the separateness of their histories, the two nations nevertheless share a mixed legacy. Both have suffered greatly at the hands of stronger neighbors, yet both have engaged in heroic national struggles that have uplifted their collective self-images and generated well-deserved pride in their accomplishments. Politically, they share a mixed legacy as well. Democratic tendencies rooted in generations of relative social equality vie with the authoritarian strains of the imperial past, clerical populism, and bolshevism. It has often been said that the lack of a national nobility in the modern era has given Czech and Slovak society an inherent egalitarianism; yet it must be added that even within the awakening societies of the late Habsburg era, democratic tendencies competed with the inherent inequality between the industrial worker and the urban intellectual, or between the peasant and the village priest. Modern-day Czechs and Slovaks are therefore the product of several deep polarities in their national heritages: pride and humility, dependency and independence, and democracy and authoritarianism.

NOTES

1. Imre Boba, *Moravia's History Reconsidered: A Reinterpretation of Medieval Sources* (The Hague: Martinus Nijhoff, 1971).

2. This is not to say that relations between Czechs and Germans in Bohemia were always friendly. In fact, conflicts were not uncommon, and mutual suspicions were often quite strong. To be sure that Germans would not penetrate Czech fortifications surreptitiously, the password to enter Czech towns frequently included the letter ř—a sound Germans generally could not pronounce.

3. See, e.g., Milič Čapek, "The First Contact of Czechs with Western Civilization: The Mission of St. Amand in the 7th Century," in Miloslav Rechcígl, Jr., ed., *The Czechoslovak Contribution to World Culture* (The Hague: Mouton, 1964), pp. 183–201.

4. Miroslav Hroch has identified the three phases as characteristic of nationalist movements among smaller European nations generally. Hroch, *Die Vorkämpfer der nationalen Bewegung bei den kleinen Völkern Europas* (Prague: Acta Universitatis Carolinae Philosophica et Historica, Monographia 24, 1968).

5. These surveys are discussed by Archie Brown and Gordon

Wightman, "Czechoslovakia: Revival and Retreat," in Archie Brown and Jack Gray, eds., *Political Culture and Political Change in Communist States* (London: Macmillan & Co., and New York: Holmes and Meier, 1977), pp. 163–170. Some of the surveys are reported in Jaroslaw A. Piekalkiewicz, *Public Opinion Polling in Czechoslovakia, 1968–1969: Results and Analysis of Surveys Conducted During the Dubček Era* (New York: Praeger Publishers, 1972).

6. Pavel Tigrid, "The Prague Coup of 1948: The Elegant Takeover," in Thomas T. Hammond, ed., *The Anatomy of Communist Takeovers* (New Haven, Conn.: Yale University Press, 1975), pp. 399–432.

2

History, Geopolitics, and Czechoslovakia's International Position

Czechoslovakia's international position is the product of obdurate historical and geographical realities endlessly woven together. The country's location at the crossroads of Europe has facilitated a mixing and blending of different cultural influences, and yet the society that has been left in the wake of those crosscurrents has evolved its own distinct characteristics. Always existing under the threat of more powerful outsiders, Czechs and Slovaks have maintained their separate national identities and resisted assimilation into the neighboring cultures. Themselves never a serious threat to others, their position in European diplomacy has been a defensive one, and because of the proximity of aggressive powers, their defense has always been dependent on friendly allies who they hoped would come to their aid in times of crisis. Given their location in the center of Europe, it was quite predictable that crises would recur.

In addition to its location, Czechoslovakia's size is another vital factor in the evolution of its international position. With 49,370 square miles of territory and about 15 million people, Czechoslovakia is roughly comparable to the state of Illinois—more populous than Illinois but slightly smaller in size. Perhaps one can begin to understand the implications of these statistics by remembering that almost any Czech could leave his home and arrive at any of four international borders within a three-hour drive. More to the point, the entire population of Czechoslovakia is much smaller than the number of Soviet citizens killed during World War II. In economic terms, Czechoslovakia is relatively advanced as compared to most other socialist countries, but its gross national product is exceeded by that of several American states.

Like most small nations, Czechs and Slovaks must inevitably perceive themselves as weaklings in the sometimes deadly game of world politics, and their long history of defeat and submission only serves to reinforce that self-impression. Located in the heart of what was for many centuries an unstable continent, Czechoslovakia has long been buffeted by the tides of great-power conflict. The proud heritage of national struggle is of some compensation to the collective self-image, but it is counterbalanced by a profound consciousness of weakness.

THE PLIGHT OF SMALL COUNTRIES

The modern world is composed of some 150 or more states ranging in size from Vatican City to the Soviet Union. The majority of today's independent states are small, weak, economically backward, or characterized by some combination of these attributes. Traditionally, world politics has been dominated by larger powers—Great Britain, France, Germany, Imperial China—and, in the years following World War II, by the United States and the Soviet Union. Recently the ability of the two postwar superpowers to control global affairs has been challenged by some smaller states, but it is clear that a hierarchy of power still exists among the countries of the world.

Throughout history, relatively small and weak countries have been persistently threatened by larger and mightier states. Most smaller states have been repeatedly conquered and subdued by stronger neighbors. Some, like Latvia, have been independent only at exceptional moments; others, like Vietnam, have been almost perpetually engaged in a struggle for independence. Still others, such as modern Finland, have been sovereign within certain political conditions determined by a powerful neighbor (in this instance, the USSR).

The geographical location of modern Czechoslovakia has been a critical factor in its development, just as it was in the development of Bohemia and Slovakia earlier. The Kingdom of

Bohemia was rimmed by mountains on three sides; these were sufficiently rugged to offer protection from most outside forces in the Middle Ages and into the early modern period, but the terrain did not stop the Habsburgs in the seventeenth century—much less Hitler in the twentieth. Slovakia was easily penetrated from the south in the tenth century and thereafter, despite the fact that mountainous terrain in the north and east effectively protected against invasions from those directions until the mid-twentieth century. (It was only with difficulty that the Soviet army, aided by Slovak partisans familiar with the terrain, broke through German defenses in eastern Slovakia in 1944–45.) Thus in no way can it be said that Czechoslovakia enjoys the natural protection of a Switzerland.

Czechs and Slovaks have always been caught up in the volatile history of east-central Europe. They have seen many wars, a procession of empires, and frequent conflict among the peoples that have inhabited or passed through the region. Entire communities, for example the Avars, have vanished amid the violent events; others, such as the Sorbs of Lusatia, have retained only the barest elements of a distinct culture. The small nations that have flourished, declined, and reemerged— as have the Czechs and Slovaks—have done so against great odds. Simply to have survived as a community is no mean accomplishment in this part of the world.

BETWEEN GERMANY AND RUSSIA

There is a widespread consciousness among Czechs and Slovaks that their national existence is quite insecure. The Czech novelist Milan Kundera expressed this thought well in 1967 when he said, "There has never been anything self-evident about the existence of the Czech nation."[1] During the long period of darkness, both the Czech and Slovak national cultures nearly suffered the fate of the Avars or the Sorbs. Habsburgs and Hungarians dominated Czechs and Slovaks thoroughly —one might have thought irresistibly. German culture seemed so much more elevated than Czech, Hungarian so much more than Slovak. With strong aristocracies supporting the development of the dominant culture, Czechs and Slovaks might simply have been absorbed into the more powerful cultures of their rulers. That they were not is perhaps partly attributable to historical happenstance, specifically the policies of the Habsburg rulers Maria Theresa and Joseph II (policies that diminished the powers of church and nobility and encouraged Protestantism).

More important, however, is the fact that the national cultures were nurtured through the centuries of darkness by the peasantry, who kept alive their native languages, folk traditions, popular art and music, and oral history. When the intellectuals of the nineteenth century set about recreating a national "high" culture, they consciously built upon the long-preserved foundations of the popular culture. Folk themes, for example, are easily recognizable in the music of the Czech composers Bedřich Smetana and Antonín Dvořák, familiar throughout the world, and also in the literary works of Kollár, Mácha, and the late-nineteenth-century Slovak poet Svetozar Hurban-Vajanský. To a modern Czech or Slovak, the national heritage is especially precious because of its deep and clear connection to the common people.

Traditionally, of course, the primary threat came from Germany and Hungary. The bitterest cultural conflict actually developed during the late nineteenth century between Slovaks and Hungarians. Prior to that time, interaction between the Slovaks and their rulers had been relatively limited, because most Slovaks lived in the remote villages of northern Hungary's uplands. In the nineteenth century, Slovaks began to drift southward out of the mountains and into the lowlands, where they came into greater contact with the Hungarians. This demographic pattern was intensified after 1867, as industry developed in the lowlands. In the conditions of the Dual Monarchy, Hungarian control over the political and administrative apparatus was nearly absolute. Social and economic conflict grew between Slovaks and Hungarians, and the government polarized the situation by enforcing measures aimed at ethnic assimilation. As Slovak nationalism grew and converged with the Czechs' movement, the conflict with the Hungarians intensified. By 1914, the result was a sharp confrontation in which the Hungarian ruling class looked with extreme suspicion upon every manifestation of Slovak culture and, in its overzealous efforts to preserve its rule, sought to destroy the basis of Slovak nationalism.

The Czech-German confrontation had a longer history, more varied in its intensity and at times ambiguous. The German colonists invited into Bohemia by the Přemyslid and Luxemburg kings were welcome settlers who contributed to the growth of the kingdom's prosperity; their coexistence with Czechs was not always without conflict, but neither was it a major source of instability. When the Habsburgs extinguished the Bohemian revolt of 1618–20 and swallowed up the crownlands, they did so not as Germans against Slavs but rather as Catholics against Protestants. Indeed, the "Winter King" Frederick who led Bohemia at its moment of defeat was himself a German prince. It was only after the Germanization of the Habsburg Empire by Joseph II and with the development of a Czech nationalist movement that nationalism itself became the dominant issue in the conflict. It was not until Hitler that any German-speaking ruler consciously sought to obliterate Czech national culture. Nonetheless, the greatest threat to the survival of that culture may not have been in the twentieth century but rather in the seventeenth, when, in the name of religion, the precocious culture of Bohemia was stifled by the excesses of the Counter-Reformation. In retrospect it seems almost miraculous that Czech culture was not snuffed out permanently. Instead, it reemerged in the nineteenth century as a modern national culture.

In the first half of the twentieth century, Czech national culture once again came under a direct and intense peril. Had Germany's bid for control over east-central Europe not been thwarted in 1914–18, it is difficult to say whether Czech culture would have flourished or declined. As it turned out, Czech culture blossomed in the independent First Republic, only to be mortally threatened once again by the Nazi tide. Hitler made no secret of his disdain for Czech culture; his long-range goals included the genetic assimilation of Czechs into German society. The German threat extended to the Slovaks as well: The nominally independent Slovak wartime state was in reality a convenient instrument of Hitler's larger purposes, as Hitler was certainly no connoisseur of Slovak culture and no admirer of

Slovak nationalism. He tolerated the ultranationalist trappings of Tiso's state only as long as they conformed to his grander design. His influence on the development of Slovakia encouraged the ugliest impulses in the nation's make-up—fascist extremism, anti-Semitism, xenophobia—and suppressed the nobler aspects of the Slovak character.

Germany's total defeat effectively ended the menace from the west, but the Soviet victory ushered in a new source of influence. Czechs and Slovaks had long been cognizant of Russian culture, and many of their greatest national leaders had been attracted by the Pan-Slavic notion of a brotherly affinity between themselves and the largest member of the Slavic family. Though rejected by Masaryk, Pan-Slavism had a strong influence on some other national leaders such as Karel Kramář. Among the Slovak awakeners, Pan-Slavism had an even stronger appeal; Kollár and Štúr accepted Pan-Slavism, as did their contemporary Ján Hollý and an entire generation of National Party figures at the end of the nineteenth century. Half a century later, the Pan-Slavic ideal would seem to have taken on a twentieth-century version in Beneš's eagerness to trust his country's security to Soviet Russia.

Despite the long strain of Pan-Slavism in intellectual circles, real connections between Czechoslovakia and Russia were not well developed prior to 1945. The one major exception had been the adventures in 1917 of the Czechoslovak Legion, whose high-water mark was reached between the February and October revolutions, that is, during the ephemeral rule of the provisional government. With the triumph of the Bolsheviks and the withdrawal of Russia from the war, this connection was interrupted; some of the legionnaires ended up fighting against the new Soviet government, thereby souring relations between the Bolsheviks and the soon-to-be-born Czechoslovakia. Nor did the Czechoslovak-Soviet treaty of 1935 reflect any mutual love. Rather, it reflected nothing more than a common interest in defense against the rising forces of fascism.

When the Soviet army moved into Czechoslovakia and drove the Germans out in 1944–45, the Soviets were accepted with much ambivalence. On the one hand, there were incidents of excessive brutality, looting, and rape as the liberators moved across Slovakia. Catholics had good reason to believe their priests' warnings about godless bolshevism, and democrats, by and large, were under no illusions about the character of the liberators' own government. On the other hand, the liberation was welcomed by many Slovaks and a great many more Czechs. The German yoke had been very heavy, and it was with great relief that it was thrown off. So great was the enthusiasm of some Czechs that there were rumors of fathers who were proud to offer their maiden daughters for the pleasure of the Russian soldiers. Beneš himself accepted the Soviets as essential backers of the new order in east-central Europe. Apparently believing in a kind of convergence theory, Beneš hoped that the Soviet system would evolve in a democratic direction—and, therefore, that any likely influences upon his own country would be positive.

The experience of 1945–48 proved to be very disillusioning, and the events following the Communist takeover still more so. The Soviet army stayed in Czechoslovakia only until 1946, but it participated pointedly in the reorganization of local government, the militia, and the Czechoslovak army. Soviet diplomatic influence was felt very bluntly in Prague well before February 1948, as, for example, in 1947 when Soviet pressure caused Gottwald's cabinet to reverse its position and withdraw from the American-sponsored Marshall Plan. Somewhat later, Prague also abandoned ongoing negotiations with the French concerning a new treaty. In the critical moments of the 1948 crisis, the USSR's deputy foreign minister, Valerian Zorin, arrived in Prague to underscore his government's interest in the outcome of events. It is not certain that Soviet pressure directly brought about Beneš's capitulation to the Communists, but it was clear that the president's desire not to disturb the alliance was of paramount importance. After "victorious February," the Soviet influence would become not only decisive but increasingly more in the nature of directives than advice.

IN THE SOVIET ORBIT

Beneš's dream that Czechoslovakia would be a bridge between East and West was unrealistic in the context of the postwar era. The cold war was well underway by 1948; Europe was being divided into two opposing camps, and Czechoslovakia was forced to take a stand. The West, for its part, had displayed a lack of willpower in 1938, an ambivalence toward Czechoslovakia in 1945, and an unwillingness in February 1948 to be drawn into the political crisis. The Communist takeover, together with the resignation of Beneš and the death of the pro-Western Jan Masaryk, ended all notions of a balanced foreign policy and affirmed that Soviet power would be the foundation of Czechoslovakia's international orientation.

The Stalinist Era

The predisposition of the country's leadership after 1948 solidified the deepening ties with Moscow. Klement Gottwald, who assumed the presidency upon Beneš's resignation, saw no essential difference between the national interest of Czechoslovakia and the common interest of the emerging socialist bloc. He had been head of the Czechoslovak Communist Party since 1929, when his forces had captured the Party's leadership and drawn it into a close relationship with the Soviet-led Comintern. During the Second World War, Gottwald's exile in the USSR had brought him even closer to Stalin, and there can be no doubt that he consulted the Soviet leader regularly during this time on questions of political tactics. After his return to Czechoslovakia, Gottwald kept in touch with the leading Soviet representatives in Prague, who served as Stalin's intermediaries. It is probably inaccurate to say that Stalin and Gottwald had a detailed plan for the takeover of Czechoslovakia, but it is indisputable that Gottwald's brilliant maneuvering was partly attributable to the expert coaching of Soviet advisers. Gottwald thus played a role similar to that of other postwar East European leaders such as Poland's Bolesław Bierut, East Germany's Walter Ulbricht, and Hungary's Mátyás Rákosi: he led his country into a Soviet-style Communist order at home while cementing political, economic, and military ties with the USSR. The exact nature of these ties took shape with the evolution of the new Communist Information Bureau (Cominform), founded in 1947.

Just as Gottwald saw the interests of Czechoslovakia to be

identical to those of the socialist bloc, Stalin saw the interests
of the bloc as synonymous with those of the Soviet Union. In
the winter of 1947–48, Stalin's view of matters of policy and
bloc interest was challenged by President Tito of Yugoslavia. A
heated debate between the Yugoslav government and the Cominform showed that the differences were irreconcilable and culminated in Yugoslavia's expulsion from the Cominform. At
this point Stalin became urgently concerned about the solidarity
of the Eastern bloc as it confronted an increasingly unified
Western camp. He therefore acted to strengthen the instruments
of Soviet influence over Eastern Europe, turning them into a
complex and highly efficient system of political control. Cominform agents, Soviet embassy staffs, military and economic
advisers, and KGB (secret police) agents all contributed to the
tightening of Soviet control throughout the region. Subsequently, sweeping political purges were carried out with the
encouragement and advice of Stalin's representatives, resulting
in the elimination of all who were perceived to be a threat to
the realization of Soviet interests in each country.

In Czechoslovakia, as elsewhere in the bloc, the Stalinist
patterns of control set a somber tone for the development of
the socialist alliance system. It was at this time that the ominous
metaphors commonly associated with the Soviet bloc became
popular in the West: an "iron curtain" (Winston Churchill's
phrase) was drawn around the "satellite nations" in the Soviet
"orbit," separating the "captive nations" from the "free world."
Extravagant though it might seem, there was some truth in the
imagery, for in the postwar realignment of Eastern Europe, the
smaller countries did, in a sense, revolve around the Soviet
Union. The military defense of Eastern Europe became, first
and foremost, a forward arm of the Soviet defenses. Economic
planning in Eastern Europe had to take into consideration the
needs of the USSR, often with results that distorted the pattern
of domestic growth and foreign trade. Czechoslovakia, which
had done very little trading with the Soviet Union prior to 1948,
redirected its production in order to supply the Soviets with
products such as processed metals, machinery, railroad cars, and
uranium. Pricing mechanisms generally favored the Soviets,
who as a result were able to "subsidize" their country's postwar

reconstruction at the expense of Czechoslovakia and the other
smaller countries of the bloc. In this and many other respects
the Stalinist bloc resembled a new kind of empire—notwithstanding the Communists' vehement objections to the use of
that term to describe their relationship.

Politically and ideologically, the Soviets had the last word
on every important question of the day. The political systems
of Eastern Europe were modeled after that of the USSR. Economic planning was structured according to the Soviet example,
and the Stalinist strategy emphasizing capital investment and
rapid industrialization was applied uniformly throughout the
region. In culture and education, Stalinist norms also prevailed.
A rigid socialist realism permeated the arts, and educational
systems were reorganized to make room for ideological training
as well as the inculcation of a "working-class" perspective on
all aspects of knowledge. Philosophy was absorbed by Marxism-
Leninism, which in turn was a narrowly perceived body of social
doctrine rigidly contoured by Party ideologists and approved by
Stalin. The Soviet leader himself was integral to this closed
system, and he dominated his empire until his dying day.

After Stalin

Many aspects of the Communist international system have
changed since Stalin's death in 1953, yet the central fact of
Soviet dominance within Eastern Europe remains constant in
the entire post-1945 era. It is instructive to consider the changes
in the way Soviet influence has been exercised. Stalin's methods
of control were fairly straightforward. His official (Soviet)
representatives, together with the East European Communists,
formed a chain of command that connected back to Stalin
himself. Challenging the authority of the command chain was
unthinkable, and even questioning a policy line was risky. Soviet
control was exerted through both formal institutions such as
the Cominform and informal mechanisms such as the many
Soviet technical advisers. The system of power radiating out-
ward from Stalin was a specific creation of the Soviet ruler himself; his successors, who inherited his power, have managed to
keep it intact but have done so in their own ways. Today, a
more indirect chain of command still connects back to the

Soviet leadership, but there is less day-to-day interference in the domestic governance of the smaller states and more flexibility in most areas of policy. Control is more subtly exercised, on the whole, and many policy issues of general importance to the bloc are discussed multilaterally. Force can be used to resolve conflicts that appear to be beyond negotiation, but it is used sparingly and justified in terms of the alleged welfare of the whole bloc. For example, the armed intervention in Czechoslovakia in 1968, carried out in order to halt radical political reforms of which Czechoslovakia's allies disapproved, was undertaken only after alternative responses had been considered multilaterally and diplomatic pressures applied by several of the displeased allies.

Czechoslovakia had maintained a position of relative conservatism throughout the 1950s and into the 1960s. Gottwald died shortly after Stalin in 1953, prompting morbid jokes about his degree of loyalty to the Soviet chief. Gottwald's successor as Party head, Antonín Novotný, distinguished himself by resisting nearly every impulse toward political innovation whether arising from within his own country or from other socialist societies. An enormous statue of Stalin was erected in Prague some twenty months after Stalin's death, ironically at a time when the new Soviet leadership was moving carefully away from some of Stalin's main policy lines. In 1956, Novotný found himself quite in step with the bloc as he strongly supported the Soviet action thwarting Hungary's revolt and suppressed his own restless intellectuals. For the most part, however, Novotný's attitude and policies lagged behind those prevailing elsewhere in Eastern Europe. Czechoslovakia was very slow to catch the spirit of de-Stalinization; long after the release of many Stalin-era political prisoners in Hungary and Poland, for example, Czech and Slovak prisoners were still languishing in confinement. Not until the early 1960s did Novotný grudgingly embrace de-Stalinization, and then he stopped far short of adopting all the implied policies.

Novotný's conservatism on domestic issues by no means reflected any serious reservations about Soviet leadership in the bloc. When economic problems forced him to approve changes in the planning structure, and when growing intellec-

ment in the 1960s began to eat away at his regime's
-, to constrain cultural freedom, Novotný's foreign policy
remained closely tied to Moscow's and showed no sign of any
deviation. This pattern was to continue even in 1968 as a new
set of leaders embarked on a thorough program of domestic
reforms, for the most part eschewing serious consideration of
similarly radical foreign policy directions. Thus even in the
turbulent year of 1968 there was no immediate challenge to
Czechoslovakia's loyal position within the Soviet bloc. In the
years since the Soviet-led intervention and the return to what is
euphemistically called "normalcy" in Czechoslovakia's domestic
affairs, the regime's loyalty to Moscow has been unquestionable.

Czechoslovakia's Contribution to the Bloc

Czechoslovakia participates fully in the formal activities
of the alliance system. The most important institutions through
which the alliance functions are the Council for Mutual Economic Assistance (CMEA), formed in 1949, and the Warsaw
Treaty Organization (WTO), the military command structure
established in 1955 as a counterpart to NATO. Neither of these
institutions was exactly meant to take the place of the Cominform, disbanded in 1956, although the informational-discussional
aspect of the Cominform has been continued through the Political Consultative Committee of the WTO. The Political Consultative Committee provides a regular forum for the member
states' top leaders to discuss important issues together. Other
than the exceptional events of 1968, Czechoslovakia has rarely
raised contentious issues within the bloc and generally accepts
the common line without quibbling.

As one of the most highly modernized countries in the
Soviet bloc, Czechoslovakia contributes substantially to the
economic and military well-being of the alliance. Nearly two-
thirds of Czechoslovakia's exports each year are destined for
its Soviet and East European allies, and a similarly high proportion of imports are purchased from other socialist countries
(see Table 2.1). Czechoslovakia's contributions to trade within
the CMEA community include large quantities of finished
products, machinery, and automobiles, as well as technical
assistance in the construction of large-scale works such as power

TABLE 2.1
Czechoslovakia's Foreign Trade, 1960-1977

Exports: Per Cent of Total According to Destination[a]

	1960	1965	1970	1975	1978[b]
Soviet Union	34.2	38.1	32.2	32.7	34.4
Eastern Europe	29.1	29.4	32.0	32.1	33.1
Developed Countries	17.4	17.4	20.6	20.5	18.9
Third World	10.4	9.5	8.7	8.7	7.9
Value of Total Exports, in current U.S. dollars (millions)	1,929	2,688	3,792	8,158	11,494

Imports: Per Cent of Total According to Origin[a]

	1960	1965	1970	1975	1978[b]
Soviet Union	34.7	35.7	32.7	31.8	35.9
Eastern Europe	28.9	31.8	30.4	32.0	32.1
Developed Countries	19.8	19.2	24.8	25.3	23.2
Third World	8.9	7.4	5.8	5.6	4.7
Value of Total Imports, in current U.S. dollars (millions)	1,816	2,673	3,695	8,874	12,210

Source: U.S. Central Intelligence Agency, Handbook of Economic Statistics 1979 (Washington, D.C.: Government Printing Office, 1979), pp.
106-07.

[a]Percentage totals do not add up to 100 because categories of destination and origin do not include all of Czechoslovakia's trading partners.

[b]Preliminary figures.

stations and chemical factories. In return, Czechoslovakia imports raw materials, fuel, food products, certain types of
machinery and equipment, and other goods.

The pattern of trade within CMEA is largely the result
of bilateral negotiations between the member states, although
a new effort at greater integration of economic development,
initiated in 1971, has increased the degree of multilateral planning. In the 1960s, Soviet Premier Khrushchev unveiled an ambitious plan to integrate the development of the bloc economies,
but it was never implemented because of Romanian objections.

The newer program is more modest than Khrushchev's plan. It has entailed increased coordination in certain aspects of national economic planning, as well as a number of cooperative programs in research and development, but it stops short of the detailed Khrushchevian vision of an international division of labor among the CMEA member countries.

For Czechoslovakia, the benefits of doing so much business with the other socialist countries would seem to be rather mixed, at best. On the positive side, Czechoslovakia enjoys a relatively dependable supply of raw materials and fuels, especially oil obtained at prices often lower than the world-market levels from the Soviet Union via the "Friendship Pipeline" that connects the USSR with Eastern Europe. In addition, Czechoslovakia's socialist allies have proved to be good dumping grounds for low-quality manufactured goods, especially consumer goods, that could not be readily sold on the world market. On the other hand, the dumping phenomenon works in both directions, obliging Czechoslovakia to accept low-quality goods from its allies. A second negative factor results from intrabloc pricing mechanisms that often dictate low prices for exports of high quality. Finally, selling so much within the bloc restricts Czechoslovakia's ability to purchase highly desired technology and high-quality goods from the West, because this limits the availability of commodities that would be salable for hard currency.

In military affairs, Czechoslovakia is again a very active partner in the WTO. The army and air force, while small in comparison to those of the Soviet Union, are important links in the WTO defense, particularly along the crucial border with West Germany (see Table 2.2). Czechoslovakia's armed forces are well trained and equipped with modern weapons. Their combat effectiveness is generally judged by Western analysts to be excellent, although a lingering popular resentment toward the Soviets since the 1968 intervention might tend to diminish that effectiveness in ways that are not overtly apparent. Five divisions of Soviet troops have been stationed in Czechoslovakia since August 1968. Initially sent in response to the political reforms of that year, the Soviet soldiers are now an integral factor in this western outpost of the WTO defenses. Their

TABLE 2.2
Czechoslovakia's Armed Forces, 1978

Army

Manpower:	140,000 on active duty
	300,000 reserves
Divisions:	5 tank divisions
	5 motor rifle divisions
	1 airborne regiment
	3 surface-to-surface missile divisions
	2 anti-tank regiments
	2 artillery brigades
	2 anti-aircraft artillery brigades

Air Force

Manpower:	46,000 on active duty
	50,000 reserves
Divisions:	13 fighter, ground-attack squadrons
	18 interceptor squadrons
	6 reconnaisance squadrons

Paramilitary Forces

10,000 border guards
120,000 militiamen (part-time)
2,500 civil defense troops

Source: International Institute for Strategic Studies, The Military Balance 1978-1979 (London, 1978).

presence in Czechoslovakia was formally sanctioned when the Prague government was forced to conclude a status-of-forces agreement with the Soviets two months after the 1968 occupation.

Long an important manufacturer of armaments, Czechoslovakia became a major supplier of arms to Third World countries in the 1950s, supporting Soviet interests in the nonaligned world. Especially significant were Czechoslovak sales to Egypt and India. Czechoslovakia's Third World arms trade diminished substantially in the 1970s, although it has perhaps been partially replaced by technical assistance furnished to certain revolutionary forces in Africa. However, the level of technical support has apparently been rather modest, probably lower than that provided by East Germany, and bears no comparison to the level of Cuban involvement in Angola, Ethiopia, and elsewhere.

An interesting novelty in Czechoslovak-Soviet relations was the naming of Czechoslovakia's first cosmonaut, Captain Vladimír Remek, to a joint space mission in 1978. Captain Remek joined Soviet veteran cosmonaut Alexei Gubarev in an eight-day flight that linked up with the orbiting station *Salyut-6* before returning to earth successfully. As the first person to be chosen from outside the USSR for one of these missions, Captain Remek—who, fortuitously, is of mixed Czech and Slovak parentage—instantly became something of a national hero.

Relations with the West

Czechoslovakia has been slow to improve its relations with the West, in contrast to the general tendency in the 1960s and 1970s of its socialist neighbors, especially Poland, Romania, and Hungary. There is evidence that the Prague government made serious advances toward West Germany in 1967, probably with the intention of seeking loans for investment in new industrial technology, but that effort was cut short by Soviet objections. In 1968, there was much discussion about the need to turn to the West for help in overcoming Czechoslovakia's economic difficulties, but again the issue was sidetracked by the occupation. It was only in 1973—well after the Soviet Union had normalized its relations with Bonn—that the Czechoslovak government was finally able to establish full diplomatic relations with West Germany.

Relations with the United States have been complicated ever since the early postwar years by two nagging problems that have yet to be resolved: American property confiscated by the Communist government, on the one hand, and Czechoslovak gold held by the United States, on the other. The confiscated American properties in Czechoslovakia have been valued at some $72 million. The gold, originally seized by Hitler's army during World War II, was captured by the U.S. army in Aachen, Germany, and has been held by the U.S. government ever since. It amounts to 18.4 tons, worth about $200 million according to world-market prices of late 1979. An agreement was reached between the two governments in 1977 whereby the gold would be returned to Czechoslovakia and Czechoslovakia would reimburse the United States for confiscated properties at the rate of forty-six cents per dollar of valuation; however, the U.S. Senate failed to ratify the agreement in 1978 and the issue remained unresolved. Complicating the matter, in addition to the terms of compensation, was public concern in the United States about violations of human rights in Czechoslovakia.

Czechoslovakia's economic difficulties in the late 1970s have driven the government to seek better ties with the West, as industrial planners found that they could not count on the Soviets for all their technological needs. Some success was achieved in 1978, when a consortium of Western banks—including four American banks—granted the Czechoslovak government a loan of $150 million to purchase new equipment and technology in order to update faltering industrial plants. This seemed to augur well for future East-West trade and aid, but by the end of the decade Czechoslovakia's unfavorable balance of trade was proving a hindrance to establishing further credit. The need for Western technology was officially acknowledged to be great, but the outlook for further improvements in Prague's relations with the capitalist world was uncertain.

OCCUPIED BY ALLIES: THE MEANING OF 1968

During the night of August 20–21, 1968, Czechoslovakia was invaded by armored troops of the Soviet Union, Poland, East Germany, Hungary, and Bulgaria. The invasion followed a protracted debate among these allies about the implications of Czechoslovakia's political reforms; Czechoslovakia's leaders had taken part in some of the discussions but had not been able to satisfy their allies' objections to their policies. The Soviets, who commanded the requisite military forces to spearhead an intervention, were the key to the allied decision and the leaders of the invasion.

The occupation of Czechoslovakia by its allies was ironic and unique, even in the context of a long history of foreign occupations; enemies had invaded the Czech and Slovak lands many times before, but never friends. (The anomaly of this circumstance was immediately recognized by many citizens who attempted to persuade the invading soldiers verbally that their incursion was the result of a misunderstanding.) The occupation brought a halt to political reforms deemed threatening by the leaders of the five countries participating in the invasion, but it also cast a dark shadow over the entire relationship between Czechoslovakia and its allies.

The events that led up to the invasion will be discussed in the next chapter, but they can be summarized here. Novotný, whose political authority had been disintegrating for several years, was replaced in January 1968 by Alexander Dubček as first secretary of the Communist Party. In the ensuing months Dubček was joined by a corps of additional new leaders: Ludvík Svoboda, who assumed the presidency following Novotný's forced resignation from this position in March; Foreign Minister Jiří Hájek; the chairman of the National Assembly, Josef Smrkovský; Prime Minister Oldřich Černík; and numerous others. The new ruling group quickly generated a momentum of change and reform in the entire political and economic system, the implications of which appeared to be quite revolutionary.[2] Changes in the system of political participation, for example, aimed at ending the arbitrary rule of a few high-ranking Party officials and introducing mechanisms for meaningful citizen inputs. In short, the driving motivation behind the reform program was the desire to create a novel type of democratic socialism, promisingly summed up in Dubček's phrase "socialism with a human face."

For Czechoslovakia's allies, the motives behind their intervention centered on their fear that the political reforms might erode the authority of the Czechoslovak Communist Party. A major lapse in the Party's authority, in turn, might lead to a weakening of Czechoslovakia's commitment to the socialist camp. Ominous comparisons were made to the Hungarian revolt twelve years earlier, when public pressure forced the ill-fated government of Imre Nagy to withdraw from the Warsaw Treaty Organization and declare its neutrality; Czechoslovakia's leaders in 1968 made no such move, but their allies were nonetheless apprehensive about Prague's loyalty. Another consideration was the effect that the Czechoslovak reforms were having upon dissident citizens in Poland, East Germany, and the Ukraine. A "spillover" effect had been clearly visible during Polish student demonstrations in March 1968, and other bloc leaders were alarmed about the possibility of similarly disturbing consequences among their own dissidents. Complicating the situation was the collapse of censorship in Czechoslovakia and the emergence of a free and outspoken press. Radio and television broadcasts, also uncensored, carried news of the events across the borders and into the living rooms of Czechoslovakia's neighbors.

It is noteworthy that Yugoslavia, socialist but nonaligned, did not participate in the occupation, nor did Albania, whose ties with the Soviet bloc had disintegrated several years before when the Albanian leadership transferred its loyalty from Moscow to Peking. More interesting was the refusal of Romania's leadership even to discuss the affair throughout 1968; Nicolae Ceauşescu, the Romanian ruler, publicly supported the right of the Czechoslovak Party to determine its own affairs and strongly criticized the five-power intervention. Both Romania and Yugoslavia mobilized troops in their border regions, just in case the other WTO leaders decided to go further and attempt to tamper with their peculiar versions of socialism.

Czechoslovakia's response to the occupation painfully recalled the country's experience thirty years earlier. The government ordered citizens not to resist the invaders, and with the exception of a relatively few violent incidents, this command was heeded. Nonviolent forms of resistance occurred, however, as the invading troops covered the country and sought to bring communications under their control.[3] In a humiliating move, several of the country's top leaders, including Dubček and Smrkovský, were arrested and flown to Moscow. Their release, following much psychological pressure and many threats, was greeted with tumultuous enthusiasm by Czechoslovak citizens, but it by no means signified the continuation of the reform momentum. Gradually they were replaced in their positions of leadership, as Party officials more subservient to Moscow jockeyed for power. In April 1969 Dubček was removed from his post as first secretary and replaced by Gustáv Husák, a man whose political stance in 1968 had been rather enigmatic but who, following the intervention, had moved into a pro-Soviet position. It was he who presided over the dismantling of the reforms and worked to resolidify his country's ties with the Soviet Union. Husák's regime has since earned the praise of Soviet leader Leonid Brezhnev, and there has been no doubt ever since about the Prague government's loyalty to the Warsaw pact.

Yet Another "Darkness"?

More than a decade after the intervention, Czechoslovakia's relations with the Soviet Union on another level remain a source of national sensitivity. Officially, the two governments are on the best of terms, and the leadership in Prague spares no laudatory words in its expressions of admiration and fidelity toward the USSR. Among the citizenry, a strikingly different attitude prevails. No one has forgotten the crushing disappointment of 1968, and few have misunderstood the political implications of their country's dependency on the Russians.

Tens of thousands of Czechs and Slovaks left their country in the wake of the Soviet-led occupation of 1968. Most of them probably intended to return as soon as political conditions became stabilized again, but few have done so. Remembering that conditions in Hungary began to improve measurably within a few years after the 1956 crisis, the Czechs and Slovaks who fled into exile in 1968–69 perhaps hoped that they would be able to return to a society "normalized" by moderate reform policies. Throughout the 1970s these hopes were unrealized. The policies of the Husák regime showed no signs of movement in the direction of the 1968 reforms, and in fact the government's own self-proclaimed "normalization" has meant the enforcement of neo-Stalinist controls. The "normalization" involved political recriminations that have excluded many of Czechoslovakia's brightest citizens from responsible positions in society because of their association with the events of 1968. The stringent policies of the Husák regime were so severe that at one point in the early 1970s Soviet Premier Brezhnev was rumored to have advised Husák to moderate his government's actions. Whether or not that rumor was true, political stabilization has resulted in the loss of many talented leaders and a generally alienated public.

An alienated public, if it is quiet, is apparently preferred to one that is stirred up, and the Soviet leaders obviously approve the current situation in comparison to that of 1968. The Husák regime has the full confidence of the Soviet Politburo, but its public support at home is very weak. Thanks to an active protest movement centered around the Charter 77 group, hopes for a new political resurgence are kept alive. As of this writing, however, the government continues to hold the line against pressures for significant reform, and the dissident movement has so far been restricted to a marginal role in society.[4]

Once again, the current situation recalls earlier periods of national oppression. Czechoslovakia is nominally independent and sovereign, yet the continuing presence of Soviet soldiers is a reminder that the country's socialist allies exercise a veto power over political affairs. The current government is made up of Czechoslovak citizens, but their policies since 1969 have demonstrated that the national interest comes second after the maintenance of harmony with the other member-states of the WTO, particularly the Soviet Union. A large part of the public seems to perceive this fact as evidence that Czechoslovakia is in a colonial relationship with the USSR.

Colonial nations generally do not love their masters, and it is safe to say that most Czechs and Slovaks today greatly resent the Russians. This in itself is an ironic twist of history, given the long tradition of Pan-Slavism among Czechs and Slovaks. Today the Russians are seen not as brother Slavs, to whom the smaller Slavic nations might look for inspiration and salvation, but rather as oppressors who have replaced the traditional enemies (Germany and Hungary). That they are able to exert control through the rule of native Czechs and Slovaks serves to differentiate the current situation in one important respect from the historical "darkness" of Habsburg rule. However, it does not alleviate the humbling reality of foreign domination so frequently found in the affairs of small nations. The events of August 1968 and thereafter have thus become the latest episode in a long chronicle of unhappy encounters between Czechoslovakia and its more powerful neighbors.

NOTES

1. Kundera spoke these words in an eloquent speech to the Fourth Congress of the Czechoslovak Writers' Union, translated and reprinted in Dušan Hamšík, *Writers Against Rulers* (New York: Vintage Books, 1971), pp. 167–177.

2. H. Gordon Skilling has emphasized the revolutionary character of the 1968 reforms in his authoritative book, *Czechoslovakia's Interrupted Revolution* (Princeton, N.J.: Princeton University Press, 1976). Of the many books that have been written about the 1968 reforms, Skilling's study is most highly recommended for its encyclopedic analysis of the complex events.

3. The clever but pathetic resistance was brilliantly documented by Czech television crews for a film that has been circulated in the West under the title *Seven Days to Remember.*

4. The activities of the Charter 77 group are discussed in the following chapter.

3

Government and Politics

The public mood in Czechoslovakia after 1945 appeared
to support revolutionary changes in one form or another, but
the scope and nature of the political changes that took place
under Communist rule surpassed anything that might have been
predicted on the basis of purely domestic trends before 1948.
Under the strong influence of the Cominform, Czechoslovakia's
Communist rulers dramatically restructured their country's
political patterns. Their model was that of the first socialist
state, the Soviet Union, and despite the many objective differences between the two countries the wisdom of the Stalinist
era dictated that the Soviet experience be a guide to the construction of socialism in every possible respect. The thoroughgoing application of the Soviet model to Czechoslovak society
had many negative effects, prompting some piecemeal reforms
in the system before 1968 and more radical changes in 1968. As
we have seen, the reforms of 1968 were stopped short by outside intervention, and the years since have seen a return to a
system that has much in common with the order of the Stalinist
era.

DEVELOPMENT OF THE COMMUNIST
POLITICAL SYSTEM

On May 9, 1948, the Communist-led parliament approved
a new constitution. Although the document contained a great
many liberal features, it also incorporated some Soviet-style
clauses apparently meant to limit civil rights. President Beneš

59

could not bring himself to sign the new constitution and chose instead to resign. In practice, the constitution quickly lost its importance as the new rulers preferred to concentrate power within the innermost circles of the Communist Party. Rival political parties, in shock and disarray since the February coup, were disposed of in various ways. The Social Democratic Party was forced to merge with the Communists. Two parties active only in the Czech lands, the Socialist Party and the People's Party, were allowed to continue in existence, but their ability to act independently was ended. The Democratic Party, which had received the largest number of votes in Slovakia in 1946, was disbanded and replaced by the insignificant Party of the Slovak Revival. Another Slovak party, the Party of Freedom, had no social basis in the first place and was allowed to continue in that situation. The National Front was maintained in form but not in substance and was brought under the Communists' total control in the course of 1948.

In this phase of development, Czechoslovakia was officially known as a "people's democracy." This term implied that the society was involved in a revolutionary transition to socialism but was not yet fully "socialist," as the Soviet Union had become in 1936. Nevertheless, the pattern of rule adopted by Czechoslovakia's leaders very much resembled the Soviet pattern. The state became an all-powerful force in society, imposing itself upon all aspects of life according to the arbitrary will of the rulers. The ruling Party became functionally indistinguishable from the state, and the constitutional instruments of state power became merely tools in the Party's exercise of rule. Within the power structure, a centralized hierarchy of command took shape, presided over by Klement Gottwald. Gottwald himself became a singularly powerful figure, particularly after the elimination of all serious contenders for rivalry through the purges that began in 1950. A cult of personality, much like that of Stalin, was purposefully built up around Gottwald by himself and his sycophantic associates.

Society felt the power of the Party-state in many ways. The economy was brought almost totally under state control as industry was nationalized and agriculture collectivized. All means of mass communication came under state control, and a rigid censorship apparatus ensured that no information was published, broadcast, or otherwise publicly disseminated unless it conformed strictly to the Party's code. Voluntary organizations were placed under the authority of the National Front, and all organized groups from trade unions to athletic clubs were required to submit to centralized rules and procedures. Because the Communist ideology looks askance at religious ideas, churches came under particular oppression. Church attendance was strongly discouraged, and religious leaders were harassed and persecuted; Archbishop Josef Beran of Prague was the first of several high-ranking churchmen to be arrested and sent to prison in 1949. Alert to the importance of political socialization, the Party-state took firm control over all formal institutions through which children learn political values and sought to inculcate positive attitudes toward socialism—especially in the schools, where the curriculum was given a heavy infusion of political propaganda, and in organized youth groups, which children were strongly encouraged to join. Adults, for their part, were exposed to heavy doses of political training at their workplaces as well as through the mass media.

Education and culture were strongly affected by the new norms. In the schools, not only were students taught the virtues of socialism, they were also told that many aspects of their national past were cause for shame. The First Republic and its great leaders, Masaryk and Beneš, were singled out for particularly derogatory treatment; Masaryk himself, whose image as "president-liberator" was warmly remembered by many Czechs and not a few Slovaks, was denounced in 1950 and thereafter as a perfidious capitalist and an enemy of the working class. Historians were required to distort Czechoslovakia's history by crediting the Bolsheviks and the Soviet Union with the greatest and most positive features in Czechoslovakia's twentieth-century development. Similarly in literature and the arts, the "bourgeois" heritage of the past was to be viewed as negative; culture was governed by political considerations and art was to be dedicated to the task of building socialism. Socialist realism was the style art and literature were to take, and at the height of the Stalinist era it became the only permissible form of socialist culture.

The most extreme phenomenon of the Stalinist years was the political purge. Czechoslovakia's rulers apparently resisted Soviet advice to initiate a purge of their own in 1949, when purges were begun in Hungary, Bulgaria, and elsewhere in Eastern Europe. Once the Czechoslovak purge began, however, it took on a scope and a level of violence unsurpassed in Eastern Europe. Between 1950 and 1954, according to one well-informed estimate, some 550,000 persons lost their party membership.[1] Hundreds were imprisoned, and some prominent long-standing Communists, including the onetime First Secretary Rudolf Slánský, were executed on false charges of treason and conspiracy. Spectacular show trials were held (similar to those in the Soviet Union in the 1930s) and many of the accused were sentenced to death, creating a wave of officially sponsored mass murder that horrified the population. Political arrests then spread throughout society as the secret police extended the wave of terror, and for a while the Soviet-trained secret police appeared to be acting independently of the government's control. Thousands of persons unconnected with politics were caught up in the diabolical tide of events, some of them destined to spend years in prisons or labor camps; many died in internment. Political crimes, real or alleged, ruined the lives of a great many people and even caused hardships for their children, who were often refused the right to higher education or stymied in their career advancement because of their parents' misfortunes. The purge and the social terror associated with it represented the most shameful episode in Czechoslovakia's history—so shameful that the Party itself later repudiated the injustices and atrocities of the early 1950s.

In contrast to events in neighboring Hungary and Poland, the basic features of the Stalinist system persisted in Czechoslovakia for some years after Stalin's death. The purge did not abate immediately but continued into 1954 when, for example, Gustáv Husák was imprisoned. Thereafter the terror gradually subsided, but the elements of the political and economic order remained for the most part unchanged. Efforts by intellectuals to stimulate reforms in 1956 were to no avail, and the new constitution adopted in 1960 seemed to certify the prevailing directions in the Party's policy. The 1960 constitution jubilantly proclaimed Czechoslovakia a socialist republic, the first of the Soviet allies to have graduated from the status of people's democracy.

Antonín Novotný, who had been first secretary of the Party since 1951 and president since 1957, occupied a position of power almost the equivalent of Gottwald's in his day, yet Novotný's position was perhaps more comparable to that of his Soviet contemporary Khrushchev than to that of either Gottwald or Stalin. By nature Novotný was conservative and jealous of his power, but he lacked the cleverness of Gottwald and, like Khrushchev, ruled over a Party that was less than monolithically unified. Cracks in his leadership appeared in the early sixties, and subtle policy changes, beginning with the rehabilitation of many purge victims, gradually transformed the nature of Novotný's authority. Pressure was felt from the intellectuals, from a sporadic but persistent student movement, from Slovak Communists dissatisfied with backward economic conditions in their part of the republic, and from economic reformers. The dissenting forces chewed away at the fabric of Party authority during the 1960s, but still the system under Novotný's leadership resisted change. The overall structure of Stalinist rule therefore did not alter fundamentally until 1968; it remained rigidly centralized, attended by a large and mulish bureaucracy, governed by dogmatic ideas, and virtually impervious to public opinion.

When Novotný fell, it was only the opening salvo in an attack by Communist reformers against all of the system's worst features. The short-lived reform program introduced in 1968 was aimed at truly fundamental changes in the political system. Within the framework of a socialist society ruled by the Communist Party, the program attempted to decentralize and democratize the authority system, introduce strong guarantees of civil liberties, reexamine the many judicial malpractices of the past and guarantee justice in the future, work out a more equitable relationship between Czechs and Slovaks, and institute a decentralized economic planning apparatus with aspects of market socialism. The program was by no means completely formulated by the time it was abandoned, but the general directions were quite clear.

The abandonment of the reform program created a serious problem in the post-1968 leadership's attempt to stake out a positive direction. Fearful that the reform forces might try to make a political comeback, the Husák regime resorted to the expulsion of some 470,000 party members, the removal of all influential people who played important roles in the events of 1968, the reimposition of censorship, and the persecution of those who have since dared to raise their voices or dip their pens in protest against the policies of the postreform period. Of all the changes introduced or planned in 1968, only one remains in effect—the federalization of the republic, dividing the land into a Czech Republic and a Slovak Republic—and even that change has been whittled down by Party centralization. In other matters, the regime's program has been largely a series of rather unimaginative responses to recurring domestic problems. Lacking a clear vision of creative political development, President Husák and his colleagues have relied on centralized control and Soviet-style approaches to policy. Today's political system is by no means as violent as that of Gottwald's day, but neither has it transcended the Stalinist traits of dogmatism, excessive bureaucratism, and isolation from public opinion.

STRUCTURAL FEATURES OF THE POLITICAL SYSTEM

Czechoslovakia's constitution of 1960, as modified by a constitutional law passed in 1968, defines the major institutional aspects of the country's government. It does not, however, spell out the details of the Communist Party's power within the system other than to describe the Party as the "leading force in state and society."

Since January 1, 1969, when the 1968 law took effect, Czechoslovakia has been a federative republic. The central government, whose capital is Prague, has exclusive jurisdiction over foreign affairs, defense, currency, the protection of the constitution, and federal legislation and administration. Separate governmental structures were created for the Czech Socialist Republic, also located in Prague, and the Slovak Socialist Republic, whose capital is Bratislava. The two constituent republics have a wide array of responsibilities in many areas such as education, culture, justice, health, trade, construction, and forest and water resources. In certain additional areas, jurisdiction is shared between the federal republic and the two constituent republics—notably the important areas of industry, agriculture, and food. The federative system was adopted rather hastily and under the pressure of the 1968 occupation, resulting in a great many ambiguities that have had to be clarified subsequently. The federalization act itself was a victory for Slovak forces (including Husák) who had long struggled for recognition of Slovakia's special interests within the republic. Ironically, however, the political "normalization" of the 1970s brought with it a strong tendency toward recentralization. As a result, the ambiguities in the constitutional law have tended to be resolved in favor of the central government's power. Nevertheless, the federal system remains basically intact as a political form reflecting the separate identities of the Czech and Slovak republics.

Governmental Institutions

The highest legislative body in Czechoslovakia is the Federal Assembly. Since 1969 this has been a bicameral institution divided into the Chamber of the People and the Chamber of Nationalities. The former chamber consists of delegates elected from legislative districts approximately divided according to population; the latter consists of an equal number of representatives from the Czech and the Slovak republics. Both are directly elected by the citizens, who receive the right to vote at the age of eighteen. The Federal Assembly elects the president of the republic, who serves as the highest executive officer for a term of five years and can be reelected. The president represents the state in all diplomatic affairs, calls the legislature into session, signs legislative bills (but does not have the authority to veto legislation), and appoints the cabinet. The cabinet is composed of the prime minister, the deputy prime ministers, and the ministers; its main function is to oversee the administration of state policies through the ministries, leaving the most important tasks of policymaking to the Party leaders. Despite the fact that the constitution assigns to the cabinet a seemingly powerful set of functions, in practice the ministers have little decisive authority and the prime minister carries nowhere near the prestige of the president.

On the level of the Czech and Slovak republics, again there is in each case an elected legislature and a cabinet. There is no single executive analogous to the federal president, but rather the top executive functions are fulfilled by elected national councils. A great many tasks are performed by the republic governments, and thus despite the fact that their powers are inferior to those of the central government, their purpose is more than merely a symbolic one.

The republics are further divided into regions, seven in the Czech republic and three in Slovakia. The regions, in turn, are divided into districts, and the latter into local communes. Five major cities have independent administrative status equivalent to that of the regions; these are Prague, Bratislava, Plzeň, Ostrava, and Brno.

At the local level, the main governing body is the National Committee. This body, consisting of members elected by direct vote for four-year terms, serves as a kind of town council with jurisdiction over many specific issues of concern to the locality— streets, sewers, the administration of housing codes, and so on. The committees may consist of as few as 10 or as many as 100 or more members; they are led by a chairman and a council, who also play the role of go-between in the relations between local committees and the higher state authorities.

The National Front

Political activities throughout Czechoslovakia are organized and controlled by the National Front. Formed in 1945 to coordinate the policies of the parties that governed in coalition until 1948, the National Front became subordinate to the Communist Party after the February coup and has remained so ever since. Under Communist rule, the National Front has taken on a highly structured, umbrellalike framework under which all mass organizations are obliged to find their home. Leadership within the front is drawn from the top representatives of the various organizations operating under its supervision, such as the trade unions, the youth movement, women's societies, athletic clubs, and so on. Control over the front is exercised through the presidium of the Communist Party, and at all times since 1948 the chairman or one of the deputy chairmen of the front has been a member of the Party presidium as well.

The mass organizations associated with the National Front are important instruments of political communication and mobilization. All associations formed for social or recreational purposes must be approved and registered by the front, which then also has the opportunity to disseminate propaganda through the associations and, in some cases, to keep a watch on the political attitudes of members. The Revolutionary Trade Union Movement, with a membership of some 5.5 million workers, is the largest of the organizations. The range of functions and interests encompassed by the mass organizations is very wide; among them we find such disparate entities as the Socialist Union of Youth, the Union for Cooperation with the Army, and the Czech Union of Teetotalers, as well as clubs for skiers, mountain climbers, music lovers, pet owners, and chess players.

The minor political parties still in existence are also member organizations in the National Front. These include, in the Czech lands, the People's Party and the Socialist Party, and, in Slovakia, the Party of Freedom and the Party of the Slovak Revival. None of these groups functions as a political party in the Western sense. Rather, all play a role supporting the Communist Party. Their memberships are limited by statute; although the two Czech parties have generally had memberships numbering more than 10,000 in recent years, neither of the two minor Slovak parties has ever had more than a few hundred members. The two minor Czech parties are represented in high government institutions and in the leadership of the National Front, but their influence is marginal. They are, as it were, given a handful of privileged positions in exchange for their loyalty to the Communist programs.

Elections

The National Front supervises elections at all levels and nominates all candidates for public office. Not all candidates are Communists, but all must have the approval of the National Front. In some cases, particularly on lower levels of government, voters may be given a choice between two candidates nominated by the front for the same position. Voters who do not care for the candidates offered for election may abstain from marking their ballots, but few do so for fear that such an expression of disapproval might be discovered by the authorities. Therefore, the candidates of the National Front regularly receive more than 99 percent of the votes cast. Despite the lack of suspense in the outcome, nearly all eligible voters turn out for elections, thanks to the thorough efforts of so-called agitation teams sent out to canvass electoral districts. The fact that voter turnout consistently exceeds 99 percent of the eligible citizenry suggests that those who do not vote are mostly incapacitated or too ill to leave their homes.

Judicial System

The judicial system is organized on the federal, republic, regional, and district levels. Justices of the supreme court are elected by the Federal Assembly. Judges in lower courts are elected by governmental bodies at the corresponding levels or by direct popular vote at the lowest level. Judges include both professional jurists and lay judges; the latter are included to add an element of popular participation in the administration of justice. There are two kinds of courts, civil and criminal. Civil courts deal with issues such as family affairs and divorce, while criminal courts are concerned with crimes and contested issues such as traffic accidents. Judgments of lower courts can be appealed once to a higher court.

Especially powerful is the office of the procurator general, who is appointed by the president and responsible to the Federal Assembly. As the top prosecuting official in Czechoslovakia, the procurator general supervises the entire system of state prosecution, and all lower procurators' offices are subordinate to the central office. It was the procurator general who prosecuted the leading defendants in the Stalinist purge trials, and today's procurator general oversees criminal actions taken against political dissidents.

Political-Military Relations

The supreme commander of the armed forces is the president of the republic, but military planning takes place for the most part within the Ministry of Defense, the armed forces' high command, and—most importantly—the councils of the Warsaw Treaty Organization. Czechoslovakia has an army and an air force but, as a landlocked country, no navy. Two years of active military service are required of all able male citizens. Czechoslovakia makes a substantial contribution to bloc defenses, as its armed forces are well trained and powerfully equipped (see discussion in Chapter 2).

Domestically, the armed forces play a role in the process of political socialization. Because every able-bodied male is subject to military conscription, he is also brought into intensive contact for two years with yet another convenient vehicle through which political training is carried out. Within the armed forces, political training is supervised by the office of the deputy commander for political affairs.

THE COMMUNIST PARTY

Without question, the Communist Party of Czechoslovakia is the country's supreme ruling force. Its authority permeates all institutions of the state, and its influence reaches into the most intimate affairs of social life. Since the "victorious February" of 1948, no other domestic force, organized or unorganized, has seriously challenged the Party's position. Only the power of external forces (Czechoslovakia's allies, especially the USSR) has succeeded in thwarting the will of the Party's top leadership councils. The Party thoroughly dominates the National Front, plays the most important roles in policymaking at all political levels, watches over the political attitudes of society, sets the tone and works out the details of economic and social development, and endeavors to engage citizens actively in the task of building an ideal society. As the supreme political and moral arbiter, the Party sets itself a herculean task in modern society, requiring a complex and pervasive institutional structure with wide-ranging functional agencies throughout the land.

Membership and Organization

The Party is a mass organization, comprising some 8–10 percent of the population. Throughout its nearly sixty years of existence, the Party's membership has fluctuated wildly, ranging from a low point of just over 30,000 in 1929 to more than 2.5 million in the months following the 1948 coup. Mass expulsions and purges commonly accompany changes of leadership or violent shifts in policy, as in 1929, when Klement Gottwald took command and sought to weed out all members whose revolutionary zeal was found to be insufficient. As already mentioned, the purges of the Stalinist era eliminated hundreds of thousands of Party members. The most recent large-scale turnover occurred between January 1969 and December 1970, as more than 25 percent of the Party's members were expelled because of their involvement in the reform activities of 1968. In the late 1970s, the party's total membership numbered approximately 1.4 million.

The basic unit of organization is the Party cell, organized mostly in local workplaces. Members on this level elect a committee, which in turn elects its own chairman; these officials have primary responsibility for directing the work of the Party cell. Connecting the local units to the top Party levels are precinct units (in large cities), city or (in rural areas) subdistrict units, and district and regional organizations. At each level, the members are elected by the units immediately below, although the candidates are carefully screened from above. Again at each level a committee is chosen; the committee elects a bureau as its executive organ and a secretariat to keep records and administer membership policies. Of particular importance is the role of the secretariat, which at each level oversees the nomination of candidates for leadership positions and watches over the attitudes of members and prospective members.

The Communist Party of Slovakia is organized as a separate unit within the Communist Party of Czechoslovakia. Institutionally, the effect is to add a layer of organization between the regional Party units and the central Party command. This is true only in Slovakia; there is no parallel institution existing in the Czech republic, and therefore the overall party structure is asymmetrical (see Figure 3.1). The Communist Party of Slovakia evolved for historical reasons: During the Second World War, when Slovakia was a separate country, the illegal Communist Party went underground and, for tactical purposes, reorganized

FIGURE 3.1
Communist Party: Organizational Structure

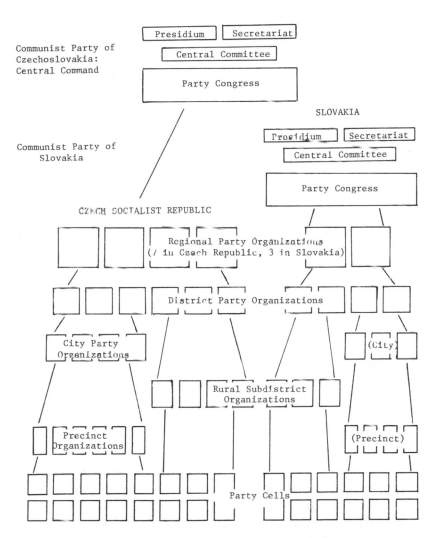

Communist Party of
Czechoslovakia:
Central Command

Communist Party of
Slovakia

as a separate political movement. When Czechoslovakia was re-united at the war's end, the Slovak Communists worked closely with the Czech Communists but insisted on retaining a separate institutional structure within the Communist Party of Czecho-slovakia. In time, this asymmetrical structure proved to be dis-advantageous for Slovaks with high political ambitions, for they found that they had to work their way through the Slovak Party before they could advance through the ranks of the cen-tral Party organization. In 1968, the question of the asym-metrical Party structure was discussed in connection with the federalization issue, but the imbalance in the Party organization was left unchanged.

At the very top level, the Party Congress is theoretically the highest Party institution. It is a large body of delegates from all over the country that meets approximately once every four years. In practice, it mainly functions to ratify general policy lines that have been decided upon by smaller Party bodies with more actual authority. One of the Party Congress's func-tions is to elect the central committee, which according to Party statutes is the most authoritative body operating between sessions of the Party Congress. However, actual power tends to concentrate in the presidium of the central committee and the secretariat, both of which are in theory elected by the central committee but in practice self-appointed. These two small groups of Party officials, together comprising no more than twenty persons, make the most important policy decisions, shape the general outlines (and sometimes the specific details) of legis-lation to be enacted by the Federal Assembly, and generally oversee the workings of the country's entire political system.

At the pinnacle of the power structure, the most important single position is that of the Party's general secretary. Gustáv Husák, who occupies not only that position but also (since 1975) the presidency, has followed in the footsteps of Antonín Novotný and made himself into a rather formidable leader. He is by no means a dictator, however, and must share his power to a considerable degree with other top officials. Ľubomír Štrougal, federal prime minister and Party presidium member, is perhaps next most powerful; Štrougal's star rose during the 1970s, and by 1979 he was being widely mentioned as the likely successor to the aging Husák.

The central governing principle underlying Party organization is the Leninist concept of democratic centralism. In theory,
democratic centralism means the free and critical discussion of
alternatives within a Party unit but a solid and unanimous stand
behind policies once decisions have been made—in other words,
democratic decision making and centralized policy application.
The concept further implies an openness on the part of higher
Party units to ideas and needs articulated from below. At the
base of the Party structure, the local cadres of the Party cell
are supposed to be responsive to the will of the broader working
class, whose interests the Party is meant to serve. In practice,
there are many violations of the principle, as the centralism
aspect tends to prevail and the democratic aspect is frequently
disregarded. There is some evidence that a lively discussion of
local issues takes place here and there at the level of the Party
cell, but it is clear that the channels of communication between
lower units and higher units are often blocked or obscured. The
most important issues tend to be discussed and decided at the
higher levels of Party authority, and lower-level Party members
tend to have a limited input into the decision-making process.
The result is that communications are channeled downward
through Party channels in the form of directives that are to be
implemented by cadres whose influence on policymaking has
been marginal.

Ideology

The guiding ideology in Czechoslovak politics is Marxism-
Leninism.[2] Briefly put, the Marxist-Leninist belief system begins with Marx's theory that history is the result of a linear
development through several major phases, the central characteristic of which is class conflict. In the modern era, this development has culminated in the rise of industrial capitalism
and the polarization of class structure into two great elements,
the bourgeoisie (owners of the means of production) and the
proletariat or working class. Capitalist society has created the
means to produce unprecedented wealth, sufficient to ensure
a prosperous life for all, but wealth and power have been
monopolized by the property-owning class at the expense of
the numerically much larger working class. Marx predicted that
the proletariat would grow in size and power as the bourgeoisie,

through its characteristic competitiveness, diminished. Then, in a moment of violent upheaval, the workers would throw off the yoke of their oppression, wrest power from the bourgeoisie, rid society of class distinctions, and build a new order. The new order, Marx further predicted, would be a socialist system; that is, the means of production would be collectively owned by society. The eventual outcome of workers' rule would be an evolution into communism, a stateless society of material abundance shared according to everybody's needs. Marx's ideas were taken up by Lenin, who refined them to fit Russian conditions, creating a professionalized party organization to spearhead the workers' movement. The victory of his Bolshevik Party in 1917 left a legacy for other revolutionary working class movements that included the organizational prototype of the *soviet*, or workers' council, the operational concept of democratic centralism, and the practical ruling example of the first successful socialist state. Under Lenin and Stalin, the socialist state developed into a powerful system of institutions and bureaucracies, yeilding a further legacy that was later to instruct the organization and policies of newer socialist states. Practical solutions to problems of policy and organization in the country of Lenin and Stalin were incorporated into Communist doctrine: the growth of a mass party organized on a strict hierarchical basis, the nationalization of industry and the strong role of state planning authorities in all aspects of the economy, the collectivization of agriculture, and the role of party and state in the supervision and control of social life.

Communists, of course, consider Marxism-Leninism a living ideological system, and Communist theoreticians have continued to modify the doctrines throughout the years. In the earlier schema, the revolutionary overthrow of the bourgeoisie would lead to a transitional dictatorship of the proletariat—a straightforwardly dictatorial rule by the working class over the bourgeoisie, lasting until the threat of a bourgeois counterrevolution had ended and the bourgeoisie had been destroyed. Socialism would then follow, characterized by the continued existence of a state structure and the distribution of material goods according to the workers' input ("from each according to his ability, to each according to his *work*"). From this point, society would evolve until it eventually reached the stage of communism ("from each according to his ability, to each according to his *need*"). Neither Marx nor Lenin had clearly indicated how long each of these postrevolutionary stages would last, but it is now clear that if the theory is correct in the Soviet and East European case, the evolutionary process is lengthy indeed. The arrival of communism has been postponed indefinitely, linked vaguely to the collapse of threatening capitalist states elsewhere in the world, and in recent years the notion of an additional stage has been introduced, that of "developed socialism." According to Soviet President Brezhnev, the USSR arrived at this stage, higher than socialism but still short of communism, in the 1960s; the smaller partners of the Warsaw pact will not attain this status until the late 1980s or 1990s.

Ideology pervades Czechoslovak politics thoroughly and makes itself felt in nonpolitical situations as well. Workers are warned to be vigilant against the attempts of the class enemy to subvert the progress of revolutionary social development. The class origins of a child's parents can determine whether or not the child receives a university education. Public media are carefully controlled so as to safeguard the ideological content of their communications. Posters and slogans are displayed prominently in an attempt to inspire workers in their task and to remind them of society's high-minded goals. In political life, Party activities take on ritualistic qualities as ideological jargon frequently masks reality and form obscures substance. For example, unpleasant realities are often referred to by means of abstract euphemisms: torture, in the Stalinist era, was called "administrative methods"; a government-imposed price increase is sometimes referred to as a "popularly acclaimed price adjustment"; the occupation of Czechoslovakia by its allies in 1968 was described as "fraternal aid" in combating the threat of "counterrevolution"; and the intervention into Czechoslovakia's domestic politics was undertaken in the spirit of "proletarian internationalism."[3]

Progress toward communism seems fraught with practical problems that confuse Party theorists. The problems require real-life solutions that must be explained in doctrinal terms, frequently producing apparent contradictions. In principle, contradictions pose no logical discomfort for Marxist-Leninists, who believe that reality progresses in a dialectical fashion; that is, contradictions occur naturally as successive realities negate each other and are eventually resolved in a positive synthesis. In real life, the dialectical process does not work so smoothly, and socialist society is checkered with contradictions not easily explained by doctrine. For example, the elimination of class differences should in theory have removed the basis of dissent and political opposition, yet dissent persists; Party spokesmen are obliged to explain this awkward reality by equating the dissidents with the old bourgeoisie, or by accusing them of conspiring with foreign capitalists, or by judging them to be criminal or mentally unbalanced.

Finally, ideology colors Communist conceptions of justice and poses a constraint on human rights. Justice is based not on a philosophy of universal rights but rather on the central concept of class reality. The welfare of the working class is assumed to be the highest value; its progress along the path of revolutionary development is taken to be the imperative purpose of society, to be guaranteed and defended by the judicial system. Class interest therefore transcends the rights of any individual, who can be presumed to lose his rights if his actions are judged detrimental to the interest of the working class. This notion may help to explain the great discrepancy between Communist and Western views of human rights. When a political dissenter in Czechoslovakia is arrested for handing out protest literature, he is being punished for actions allegedly detrimental to the interest of the working class. It does not matter that the dissenter may believe himself to be upholding the class interest and simply criticizing the Party for mistakes; the Party is presumed to be the sole arbiter of the class interest, and to challenge the Party's right to make judgments about that interest is presumed equivalent to attacking the working class itself.

Political Socialization and Control

Communists believe that socialist society provides an environment in which a new man will evolve, a man who is selflessly dedicated to the social good, trusts in the Party's leader-

ship, and works hard to realize the goals of socialist construction. To facilitate the development of the new socialist man,
the Czechoslovak regime has invested heavily in measures that
control the process of political socialization. Schools at all levels
teach Marxism-Leninism as required courses, and instructional
materials in other subjects frequently drive home political
messages. Organizations for children and young adults, such as
the Young Pioneers (for children to age fifteen) and the Socialist
Union of Youth (for teen-agers and young adults), mix strong
doses of political education with their service and recreational
activities. In addition, the Party sees to it that adults are given
plenty of opportunities to continue their political education
through the auspices of the National Front organizations. The
trade unions are active in adult socialization programs, as are
other mass organizations including the Czechoslovak-Soviet
Friendship League, the Circles of Cultural Creativity, and the
Society for the Dissemination of Political and Scientific Knowledge. For Party members, evening schools offer courses in
Marxism-Leninism, and special Party schools cater to especially
diligent members. Political socialization for both young and old
is further facilitated by state control over the mass media, for
newspapers, magazines, radio, and especially television are effective instruments for carrying political messages into the daily
lives of Czechs and Slovaks.

Notwithstanding the constant and omnipresent influence
of the regime, there is much evidence that the socialization
efforts fall short of their intended purpose. Political cynicism
is widespread, and much grumbling can be heard in private conversations about the government and the economy. On the job,
absenteeism is high and productivity is low. Many citizens
avoid attendance at political rallies and discussion sessions
unless their jobs or their children's educational opportunities
appear to be threatened by nonattendance. Political jokes
abound, and they nearly always reveal a bitter irony. (For
example, one widespread story a few years ago concerned a
naïve tourist in Prague watching automatic shovels dig a vast
hole in the middle of the city. When a local resident came
along, the tourist stopped him and asked if this was where the
new subway would come through. "No," the Czech replied,

"actually, they're digging to see how deep the roots of socialism go.")

Perhaps the strongest evidence indicating that political socialization has not succeeded is the continuing pervasiveness of social controls. The secret police are very active, and citizens are wary of strangers and even acquaintances who might be police agents. The role of the secret police is by no means as horrifying as it was during the early 1950s, but it is enough to make people cautious in the expression of their political opinions. More subtle forms of control supplement the activities of the police. Schoolteachers are often known to watch their pupils' behavior for evidence of political attitudes, and they can aid or hinder a student's prospects of admission to gymnasium (high school) or college depending on whether or not the proper attitude is displayed. On the job, workers must be careful of informers whose negative reports can jeopardize career advancement. Citizens are conditioned to these controls and usually know how to stay out of trouble, but avoiding problems entails a constant alertness and the ability to restrain one's behavior in the presence of anyone who is not known to be trustworthy.

Contact with foreigners is one of the most sensitive areas in which the regime's controls affect the public. The regime regards Westerners with suspicion, fearing that they might spread subversive "bourgeois" ideas. Tourism is encouraged—the government is anxious to have Westerners spend their hard currency in hotels, restaurants, and gift shops—but Westerners are not encouraged to fraternize with private citizens. Citizens, for their part, are expected to report to the officials all contacts with foreigners; many do not comply with this requirement, but a good deal of uneasiness attends noncompliance. As far as travel abroad on the part of Czechs and Slovaks is concerned, here again there are tight controls. Citizens wishing to leave the country must obtain permission to leave and to return in advance of their departure. The process is troublesome and time-consuming, and one is never certain that the permission will be granted. In recent years it has been impossible for the average citizen to visit capitalist countries more frequently than once in every three or four years except for professionally related trips. It is very rare that more than one member of a family will be allowed to go to the West at the same time. When an individual goes West, therefore, he is generally obliged to leave his family behind as a kind of ransom, lest he be tempted to defect.

The persistence of social controls thus suggests that the regime has little confidence in the political reliability of its citizens. By resorting to controls, the state seems to be admitting that its efforts at political socialization have not succeeded and that there has been little progress toward the development of the new socialist man.

MEMORIES OF THE "PRAGUE SPRING"

The current political reality, in which the Party rules arbitrarily and through the threat of coercion, renders the memory of the 1968 "Prague Spring" especially bitter. In 1968, the reformers who were temporarily in command of the Party and state sought to bring the regime in touch with the public and to make the government responsive to popular sentiment. What ensued upon the first steps by the new leadership was a thoroughgoing discussion of the entire political system a discussion that became increasingly open as the mass media boldly broke away from the censors' control. As the Party and government made plans to reform the ruling structure, political grouping took place among the public. Led by brilliant and articulate spokesmen, many citizens joined in the discussions in order to express deeply felt needs and raise issues important to them. The far-reaching implications of these events became apparent in the springtime, and the most important activities centered on the capital city: hence the term "Prague Spring," a popular synecdoche for the complex and exciting political changes that spread throughout the entire country and lasted well into the summer and beyond the invasion. It was a time of great public enthusiasm, for the breakdown of the Party's dictatorship created an atmosphere of freedom. It was also a time for serious work, as the Party encouraged public participation in the discussions about democratizing the political system.

Out of the discussions and initial reforms emerged a new

model of socialism. Dubček's phrase "socialism with a human face" was not merely a new euphemism for old policies; it symbolized the Party's sincere efforts to humanize the political system and to find workable remedies for the fundamental illnesses caused by twenty years of arbitrary rule. In the top ranks of the Party, opinions were divided as to the best solutions to the various problems, and definite policy lines were still being debated when the troops of the Warsaw pact intervened late in August. Nonetheless, the very issues that were being debated—and the fact that they were being discussed openly with the public encouraged to join in—made it clear that the political reality had already changed radically. Public expectations were quite high that further changes would institutionalize the tendency toward greater democracy, pluralism, and freedom.

Issues in the Reform Movement

Four broad issues became the subject of discussion as the reform leadership attempted to develop Czechoslovakia's new model of socialism. These were: the overall question of political structure and participation, justice and civil liberties, the problem of Czech-Slovak relations, and the structure of economic planning and organization. The economic issue will not be treated here but will be taken up in the next chapter. As for Czech-Slovak relations, it has already been mentioned that this question was resolved by the adoption of a federal system, a reform that has remained intact to this day. Despite the fact that the federal system is flawed, it represents a significant change, climaxing the Slovaks' long struggle for recognition within Czechoslovakia as a distinct nation.

Political Structure and Participation. While policy discussions went on, changes in the actual political processes took place. The Party's central committee adopted an action program in April that outlined some first steps toward constructing a "Czechoslovak way to socialism." The program called for enhancing the role of elected state bodies, encouraged non-Communist intellectuals and technical experts to assume more responsible roles in industry and education, acknowledged the value of cultural freedom, and suggested that some new arrangement for sharing power within the National Front might be worked out. These were rather unspecific initiatives, but they prompted an immediate response. The cabinet and parliament (then consisting only of the National Assembly) began to function independently, and new signs of life appeared in the National Front as leaders of the minor parties in particular hoped to see their organizations given a more substantial role. Radical ideas about restructuring political participation captured the public's attention. One such idea was articulated by a member of the secretariat of the central committee, Zdeněk Mlynář, who advocated the creation of an institutional system that would represent competing interest groups within the power structure of the state. The question of political pluralism was thus opened at the highest levels, and voices were heard that called for the return of a multiparty system. Few Party leaders were willing to consider the idea of opposition parties in any formal sense, but many were open to Mlynář's more moderate approach to pluralism.

Among the new organizations that formed spontaneously, mention must be made of one named the Club of Committed Nonpartisans (Klub angažoviných nestraníků—KAN). KAN was founded to organize people for political discussion and action who wished to remain outside the regular Party and National Front circles. It turned into a lively association with branches sprouting up in many localities. It was illegal in the technical sense (because it was never registered with the National Front) but it worked to establish itself as a force for change and democracy.

Within the Communist Party, the reformers' attention focused on guaranteeing freer policy debates, democratic election of officers, rotation of official positions, the independence of lower party organs, and open lines of communication. A draft statute was prepared several months before it was to be considered by the Fourteenth Party Congress, scheduled for September 1968. The draft became the focal point of a heated debate between Party reformers and conservatives, the latter seeing the proposed changes as a threat to Party discipline and central authority. As it turned out, the changes were never formally adopted, but everyday Party life reflected a sensitivity to the prevailing spirit of reform as Party organizations on all levels became the scene of lively discussions. To be sure,

many hard-line Communists opposed the new openness within
the Party, but their opposition served only to slow the tide of
democratization, not to stem it.

Justice and Civil Liberties. One of the most startling events
of 1968 was the movement to rehabilitate all the victims of
past injustices once and for all and to seek ways by which the
horrors of the past could never be repeated. A commission
headed by Jan Piller, a member of the Party presidium, investi-
gated the purge trials of the 1950s and made a number of rec-
ommendations, including the full rehabilitation of all persons
unjustly punished. The Piller commission further advised that
only by dispersing the power concentrated in central Party
organs and creating a system with plural checks and balances
could the judicial wrongs be prevented in the future. Toward
the end of June, the National Assembly gave substance to the
first of these intentions by passing a law on the rehabilitation
of the victims of past purges and persecutions.

These events signaled that the Party officially deplored
the Stalinist atrocities. Because this matter, like others, was
discussed openly, the public and the media were encouraged
to probe the past along with the Party. A remarkable new
organization sprang up, called K-231 (Club 231); this was an
association of people who had been imprisoned under the 1948
law (number 231) that had set the political arrests in motion.
In related areas, the news media explored many long-simmering
issues of the past such as the mysterious death of Jan Masaryk
and the role of the Soviet KGB (secret police) in Czechoslovakia.
All these developments seemed quite consistent with the idea
of a "socialism with a human face," and together they contributed to the new political model that was being constructed
in 1968. Whatever form that model might ultimately have
taken, it was clear that it was to be based on concepts of legality,
humaneness, and political ethics that were unique in the Soviet
bloc.

Public Activism and the Intervention

By midsummer, Czechoslovakia no longer resembled the
neighboring Communist states. The secret police had virtually
disappeared, the mass media were operating under the protec-

tion of a new law confirming the removal of censorship, political issues were being debated openly both within the Party and on the outside, new organizations were forming and operating freely, and citizens were being allowed to travel abroad at will. Society was feeling an electrifying air of change and renewal. Intellectuals were free to explore their ideas without fear of being criticized or punished for thinking improper thoughts. In this atmosphere, pressures built up within society for even more change; all the talk of pluralism and interest groups stimulated the most active citizens to generate political demands. The boldest example of these pressures occurred at the end of June, when a large group of intellectuals and workers issued a statement known as the Two Thousand Words. The statement, published in several major Czech newspapers, had been written by the talented novelist Ludvík Vaculík. It approved the Party's democratization movement but warned of the danger from conservative forces, and it called for increased efforts to realize the promise of the reform program. It called upon citizens to strengthen their activities to ensure that there would be no backsliding in the movement toward democracy and warned that it might be necessary to resist pressures from outside Czechoslovakia "if necessary, with arms."

It was fear of this public activation, perhaps as much as anything else, that alarmed Czechoslovakia's allies. The new political realities suggested a slippage in the Party's control over the public and, from the Soviet point of view, the passing of political initiative from the Party to unpredictable forces in mass society. News of the events in Czechoslovakia was reaching the workers in East Germany, Poland, and the Soviet Ukraine, and it was feared that pressures for similar changes might begin to build in these countries. (In fact, this had already occurred during Polish student demonstrations several months earlier.) The Soviets' ultimate fear was that "counterrevolutionary" forces would gain the upper hand and pressure the Prague government into revising or even realigning its foreign policy, thereby weakening the Warsaw pact's security network and splitting the bloc politically. Several months of almost unrelenting pressure, accompanied by frequent veiled threats of military action, had failed to have the desired effect on the Czechoslovak government, and last-ditch meetings—between the Soviet and Czechoslovak presidiums at Čierná-nad-Tisou in Slovakia, July 31–August 1, and with other bloc leaders in Bratislava, August 3—similarly failed to reconcile the differences. The five hard-line allies therefore concluded that military intervention was necessary to reverse the threatening trends in Czechoslovakia before they went too far.

"Normalization" and Renewed Dissent

The fact that Dubček and numerous other reformers remained in their positions for eight months after the intervention illustrates the confusion and uncertainty of both the perpetrators and the victims of the August 21 invasion. No doubt, the Soviets had expected to see the reform government crumble under the impact of occupation, to be replaced by a ready political force more congenial to the interests of the invading allies. There were of course many in the Czechoslovak Party who were willing to oblige, but the dominant tendency within the ruling circles was to stick with the Dubček group and try to salvage as much of the reform program as possible. Some sacrifices were made quickly; for example, the planned Party Congress was postponed and the draft statute reforming Party operations was abandoned. Censorship was reimposed, but it was only partially enforced throughout the winter of 1968–69. Still, the impact of Soviet pressure weakened the position of the reformers and promoted the cause of conservatives.

This continuing political crisis was punctuated by a student strike in November and ongoing demonstrations during the winter. In January, a university student named Jan Palach publicly committed suicide by self-immolation, horrifying the populace and stirring up greater tension. A climax was reached following the victory of Czechoslovakia's national hockey team over their Soviet rivals; a massive demonstration took place in Prague, during which the office of the Soviet airline, Aeroflot, was vandalized. This outpouring of anti-Soviet sentiment was an excuse for the Soviets to intervene again, this time in the form of direct political pressure for the removal of Dubček.

With the fall of Dubček, the ambiguities were quickly removed from Czechoslovak politics. Gustáv Husák, the new party chief, presided over a return to tight controls, and in short order all the reforms of 1968 were abandoned—with the exception of federalization, for which Husák himself had fought hard. The gradual removal of reformers from positions of responsibility followed, along with the expulsion of many Party members. Husák eventually signed a protocol approving the occupation of his country and required other persons in positions of authority to do likewise. By the end of 1969, a number of political arrests had taken place. For several years, Husák was believed to be a moderating force among hard-liners (for example, Vasil Bil'ak, Alois Indra, and Drahomír Kolder) who wished to see Dubček and other top reformers arrested. They were not, however; their punishment was limited instead to removal from public life, loss of Party membership, and official disgrace. Whether or not Husák was a force for moderation, moderacy is hardly the word to describe most aspects of the "normalized" political situation. Demonstrations on the first anniversary of the invasion were put down ruthlessly by Czech and Slovak police, and sporadic incidents of protest thereafter brought on further violent recriminations. Dissenters were put on the alert that their actions were likely to land them in jail.

Scattered protests nevertheless occurred in the 1970s, mostly in the form of pamphleteering and the writing of open letters to the current leaders. The playwright Václav Havel penned one such open letter in 1975, criticizing the regime and calling for compliance with the Helsinki Declaration on human rights, to which Czechoslovakia was a signatory. Alexander Dubček also wrote an open letter, similarly criticizing the policies of "normalization" and defending his former regime's policies. Ludvík Vaculík and other notable figures were known to express similar thoughts, and although their letters were never published in the Czechoslovak press, there was widespread public awareness of the actions. Yet these expressions of dissent remained isolated cries in the wilderness of neo-Stalinist politics. It was not until the advent of the now-famous Charter 77 that a strong movement could be perceived among dissenters.

Charter 77. The circulation of a new document in January 1977 disturbed the regime considerably. Charter 77, initially signed by 240 individuals of varying occupations, chided the Party and government for their violation of the International Covenant on Civil and Political Rights, signed at the 1975 Helsinki Conference. Charter 77 challenged the regime to heed the provisions in the covenant for freedom of expression, religious freedom, nondiscriminatory educational policies, individual privacy, and the right to travel abroad freely. In time, the document was signed by some 1,000 people from many walks of life; all but a few of the signatories were from the Czech lands. A number of individuals who had been prominent in the 1960s but fell out of favor after 1968 were among the charter's first spokesmen—Václav Havel, former foreign minister Jiří Hájek, philosopher Jan Patočka, and later psychologist Jaroslav Šabata. In 1978–79 the leadership broadened to include younger persons such as Jiří Dienstbier, Václav Benda, and Zdeňa Tomínová. A genuine dissent movement was generated around the causes articulated in the charter, and dozens of follow-up documents were published and circulated clandestinely by the group. As the movement developed and picked up members from the younger generation, differences of opinion became apparent over whether or not to broaden the movement's purposes and initiate actions more radical than just the publication of legal-moral appeals.

In fact, the movement's activities have broadened. Publication activities have been expanded to include books, carbon-copied and bound in what is called the Padlock series, and numerous underground periodicals. Underground cultural activities have developed, and a small-scale version of the Polish "flying university" was founded to offer lectures and seminars on political topics. As a crude form of protection for the activists, the Committee for the Defense of the Unjustly Persecuted was established, as well as a Fund for Civic Aid. Both of these loose associations are meant to publicize cases of harassment and to give financial assistance to the victims of official persecution. By the end of the 1970s, the movement had gathered a significant momentum. It seems to have become more than just an isolated phenomenon; although it remains marginal to the political system and small in direct membership, the charter movement has caught the attention of many citizens beyond its immediate circles and inspired them to hold onto the hope that the situation might be changed.

Testimony to the vitality of the movement is the regime's nervousness about its political impact. From time to time the regime has struck out at the chartists, arresting or harassing their leaders. In May of 1979 ten of the most prominent spokesmen were rounded up by the security police and charged with having circulated "false information" detrimental to the state. Five of them—including Havel, Dienstbier, and Benda—were tried five months later and sentenced to long prison terms. The event was reminiscent of Stalin-era show trials, and the international publicity stirred up much public outrage in the West, sparking protest resolutions even from West European Communist parties. The international furor appeared to have little immediate effect on the Czechoslovak government, and the circulation of protest leaflets in Prague almost immediately after the trial indicated that the movement had by no means been stamped out.

Earlier recriminations had not succeeded in slowing down the movement's momentum, and the regime seems to be divided over whether or not to take sweeping action against all the known members of the associated groups. At the time of this writing, the chartists' system of communication continues to operate. The government continues to concentrate its efforts against the dissenters' top leaders in the hope that a movement constantly having to replace its leadership will eventually die.

Charter 77 and the Legacy of 1968

Taken out of context, Charter 77 might be written off as a fringe movement, carried on by a group of courageous but reckless individuals fighting against a well-entrenched autocracy. Remembering the history of Czechoslovakia, however, we are compelled to view the movement from another perspective. In the midst of several previous dark ages, courageous individuals raised their voices and struggled to lead their nation into the light of self-discovery. The charter movement recalls those earlier heroes who lifted the national spirit and built a new order. Reflecting the noblest aspects of their country's political tradition, the chartists are by no means alone in their desire for a democratic order; rather, they represent a significant political counterculture with a potentially large basis of support. The mass political activism of 1968 demonstrated the breadth and depth of the democratic impulse in Czechoslovakia. If the chartists have so far been unable to reignite the fires that burned during the Prague Spring, it is only because the regime's systematic repression has convinced the populace that mass action now would be not only fruitless but dangerous.

Public reticence is not the only obstacle to the dissent movement. The fact that few Slovaks are numbered among Charter 77's proponents indicates a major weakness in the movement's support base. Bitter rivalries between Czechs and Slovaks have underlain the surface all along, and in the atmosphere of "normalized" Czechoslovakia the regime is not above playing upon these rivalries to keep the potential opposition divided. As far as the regime itself is concerned, its response to the pressures of Charter 77 has been a mixture of defensiveness and retaliation. Increasingly unable or unwilling to take any progressive steps, Husák and his colleagues have kept a tight rein on their rule while avoiding any new political initiatives. Fearful of sharing power, they continue to guard their own positions jealously, thus perpetually abandoning the frontiers of political innovation to forces outside the Party. Charter 77 therefore has a continuing raison d'être.

Importantly, the ongoing dissent movement guarantees that the dreams of 1968 will not merely pass into memory. In the longer historical frame, 1968 was a link between the democratic past and the uncertain future; a whole generation of Czechs and Slovaks were reawakened to the possibilities of political freedom, and they are not likely to forget the experience. Charter 77 is an attempt to keep the reality of freedom alive, if only as a vision of what could be.[4]

CONCLUSION

The brief interlude of democratic experimentation colloquially known as the Prague Spring stands out as an extraordinary bright spot in the history of Communist Czechoslovakia. Aside from the hopeful reforms of 1968, the political system has developed quite autocratically; the Party, in theory ruling on behalf of the working class, has been largely insensitive to the aspirations of its constituency and unwilling to open itself to truly democratic participation. Thus out of step with the long tradition of Czechoslovak democracy, the Communist regime has forsaken its self-acknowledged historical mandate and created a situation in which it rules over an alienated populace. The conscience of society speaks out in the activities of dissenters such as the Charter 77 group, but the government refuses to listen and goes its own way.

The foregoing discussion of the political system has taken on an overwhelmingly negative tone. This would seem fitting, given the fact that the ruling group has consistently violated many of the political norms implicit in its guiding ideology: democratic rule by the working class, freedom of expression, and so on. However, it would be unfair to conclude this chapter without mentioning some of the positive aspects of the system. The socialist revolution carried forward earlier progress toward the elimination of social inequalities; this has by no means led to the absence of rich and poor, but the blatant extremes of poverty and wealth characteristic of advanced capitalist countries are not to be found in socialist Czechoslovakia. There is a relative equality of opportunity for citizens, marred to some extent by official prejudices against persons with unfavorable social or political backgrounds, but nevertheless offering the promise of advancement and mobility for many who had no such hopes prior to the revolution. The constitutional right to work is taken very seriously, and unemployment is virtually unknown. A comprehensive social welfare system provides a modest security against the financial uncertainties of illness, aging, and bad luck. Finally, in one area where the First Republic had failed egregiously, the two major halves of the republic have been significantly equalized: Slovakia is no longer a "poor cousin" of the Czech lands in terms of either economic development or political significance. Symbolic of this is the fact that the last two party chiefs, Dubček and Husák, are both Slovaks.

Yet one is forced back to the conclusion that the political system is predominantly characterized by negative features.

No matter how one defines democracy, it cannot be said to
exist in today's Czechoslovakia. The regime persists in ruling
from the top and ignoring the potential contribution of the
wider public. Controls over society are pervasive, and citizens
cannot travel freely. Especially since its retrenchment from the
1968 reforms, the Party has betrayed the workers' confidence
and failed to provide effective leadership. The resulting political atmosphere is one in which the public is disillusioned and
apathetic, distrustful of authority, pessimistic about the future,
and inclined to withdraw into private life rather than participate as socialist men and women in collective activities.

NOTES

1. Zbigniew K. Brzezinski, *The Soviet Bloc: Unity and Conflict*,
rev. ed. (Cambridge, Mass.: Harvard University Press, 1967), p. 97.

2. Marxist-Leninist ideology is obviously a complex subject and cannot be treated here in any detail. For a popular introductory study, see
Alfred G. Meyer, *Communism*, 3d ed. (New York: Random House, 1967).

3. Otto Ulč has referred to this peculiar language as "Stalinese,"
although in many respects the jargon of Communist officialdom bears
some resemblance to Western "bureaucratese." For Ulč's interesting discussion of political communication in Czechoslovakia, see his *Politics
in Czechoslovakia* (San Francisco: W. H. Freeman and Co., 1974),
pp. 130–140.

4. My thanks are due to H. Gordon Skilling for having impressed me
with the logic of this argument. Professor Skilling's forthcoming book
on the charter movement will make this point.

Prague: Vltava River, Charles Bridge, and Hradčany Castle.

Old Town, Prague: Hus monument (1915) with Kinský Palace (1755–1765) in the background (*above*); Týn Church (fourteenth–sixteenth century), the principal church of Prague during the Hussite era (*below*).

Rotunda of St. Martin, Prague/
Vyšehrad (eleventh century)
(*left*); Karlštejn Castle, Central
Bohemia (fourteenth century)
(*below*).

Tábor, town hall in the Renaissance style (1521) with Žižka monument in the foreground (*above*); portion of fresco depicting the legend of St. George (1338), castle of Jindřichův Hradec, South Bohemia (*below*).

Young women in festive attire of traditional
Moravian design, Šumice (Uherské Hradiště
district) (*left*); old women in peasant dresses
of traditional Moravian design, Šumice
(Uherské Hradiště district) (*below*).

Slovak folk architecture: peasant cottage, Orava district.

Bratislava Castle, Bratislava (*above*);
Slovak National Theater, Bratislava (*left*).

4

The Economy

Czechoslovakia's economy has gone through many ups and downs. Its pre–World War II capitalistic system was built upon a firm base inherited from the old Austrian order. Despite great disparities between the more developed western provinces and the backward eastern regions, the First Republic was one of the most advanced industrial states in Europe. After World War II, revolutionary changes upset and destabilized many of the established economic patterns but nevertheless made Czechoslovakia the strongest economic ally of the Soviet Union during the 1940s and 1950s. The centrally planned system achieved impressive results in overall industrial production, but chronic shortages of food and consumer goods pointed to serious problems rooted in both structural factors and management policies. Attempts to reform the system on a grand scale were frustrated by political circumstances, and piecemeal adjustments in recent years have not eradicated the fundamental difficulties. As Czechoslovakia moved into the 1980s, the outlook was one of uncertainty.

GEOGRAPHICAL AND HISTORICAL BACKGROUNDS

The development of Czechoslovakia's economy, like its history, has been influenced by its geographical setting as well as by the political realities of its Central European location. Bohemia and Moravia, blessed by much fertile farmland and favored by the investment climate of nineteenth-century Austria, have long been modern, industrial regions. Slovakia, a

generally more rugged territory that was traditionally attached
to the more backward Hungarian kingdom, lagged behind the
Czech lands in its economic development and only began to
catch up during the 1970s. In order to understand the nature
of the economic system under Communist rule, therefore,
it is necessary to take a look at the background conditions.

Land and Resources

A geographer once described Czechoslovakia as "a veritable
mosaic of physiographic units," indicating that this small country has quite a variety of different land forms.[1] Bohemia, a
diamond-shaped province, is dominated in the west by the
Bohemian Massif, a range of moderate mountains reaching altitudes exceeding 3,000 feet, and in the east by the gentler
Bohemian-Moravian Uplands. The interior regions of Bohemia
form a large basin, the surface of which is in some places rolling and in others flat. The most important river system consists
of the Labe (Elbe) and its tributaries, especially the Vltava
(Moldau), which flows through Prague. Moravia is defined largely
by the drainage basin of the Morava River, which extends also
into Slovakia. The Morava flows southward, becoming a part of
the border between Slovakia and Austria before emptying into
the Danube just north of Bratislava. To the north, Moravia is
protected by the Jeseník Mountains, a part of the Sudet range.
Slovakia is characterized by numerous mountain ranges, all a
part of the Carpathian system, capped in the north by the
craggy peaks of the High Tatras, which reach altitudes as high
as 8,711 feet. Southward-flowing tributaries of the Danube,
chiefly the Váh, Nitra, and Hron Rivers, interrupt the highlands
by carving fingerlike valleys that widen into a fertile plain ap-
proaching the Danube. Farther east the highlands are punctuated by streams that drain into the Tisa (Tisza), which itself
forms a small stretch of the borders with the Soviet Union and
Hungary.

Much of the natural character of the land has been removed or covered over by the activities of humans, but nonetheless nearly one-third of Czechoslovakia is still covered by
forests. These provide the basis for a well-developed industrial
sector that produces lumber, paper, and furniture. All forested

lands are now state-owned, and extensive efforts have been put into conserving some of the areas for recreational purposes.

Agriculture is practiced on more than one-half of the country's land surface. Variations in terrain, soil conditions, and climate render some regions very fruitful while others are only marginally productive. Wheat, barley, sugar beets, corn, and fodder crops are grown successfully in the lowlands; rye, oats, and potatoes are the main crops in the hills. On the slopes of central Slovakia's Low Tatra and Little Fatra ranges, grazing lands encourage sheep raising. Elsewhere, swine and poultry are raised in generally greater quantities than cattle. Czechoslovakia is not self-sufficient in food production and must import a number of basic commodities, especially grains and meat.

Mineral resources are not abundant, and energy sources are in short supply. Coal and lignite are the exceptions, mined mostly in the area around Ostrava in northern Moravia. Modest quantities of iron ore are extracted from a significant but dwindling source in the Ore Mountains of eastern Slovakia. Other minerals yielding marginal outputs are copper, manganese, zinc, lead, tin, mercury, antimony, and uranium. Oil and natural gas deposits are located near Hodonín in Bohemia, but they provide only a fraction of the needed supplies.

Hydroelectric capacity has been substantially increased since 1945, but it still plays a proportionally small part in the total energy picture. As a result, large supplies of fuel and energy, as well as raw materials, must be imported regularly to maintain industrial production. The chief supplier of these vital resources is the Soviet Union.

Development of the Economy to 1948

The Czechoslovak Republic inherited a wealth of already-developed industry from the old Austro-Hungarian Empire. It has been estimated that 43 percent of the total industrial labor force in pre-1914 Austria and Hungary was employed in Bohemia, Moravia, and Slovakia.[2] The Czech lands were by far more developed than Slovakia, and Ruthenia was quite undeveloped. Major industrial complexes had grown up in and around Prague, Plzeň (Pilsen), Kladno, Ostrava, Brno, and Bratislava (Pozsony); a number of lesser industrial centers in

Slovakia were also significant, such as Košice (Kassa), Ružomberok, and Žilina. Especially important in Bohemia and Moravia
was the production of coal, machine tools, chemicals, textiles,
pulp and paper, building materials, and food products, as well
as the existence of a large armaments factory, a part of the
Škoda works in Plzeň. Railroad cars and locomotives were manufactured in substantial numbers, and production of motor cars
and airplanes had also begun prior to World War I. Slovakia
did not possess such a complex and diversified industrial system
as this, but the region nevertheless was more highly developed
than many others in relatively backward Hungary. Textiles,
lumber, paper, and food products were the most important
commodities produced, but by 1914 there had also arisen some
heavier industrial concerns such as the electrochemical plants
and machine factories located mostly around Bratislava.

During the war, production declined and inflation made a
shambles of the empire's monetary system. Thanks to firm
leadership and sound economic policies, the fledgling Czechoslovak republic was able to recover quite rapidly and entered a
period of overall prosperity. The economy was of course sus-
ceptible to the ups and downs of business cycles typical of capitalist systems; the effects of the Great Depression were by no
means small, and at other times fluctuations in the market
could cause unemployment, strikes, and uncertainties for investors. As a small country dependent on international trade,
Czechoslovakia was strongly affected by trends in the world
market. Thus when foreign demands for sugar declined in the
mid-1920s, for example, lessened sales of this important export
product caused serious agricultural dislocation and tremors in
the economy as a whole. When the world depression damaged
many sectors of the export trade, the effect on the domestic
economy was very severe. Still, it seemed that Czechoslovakia's
economy weathered the storms of the interwar period better
than most neighboring countries, and on the whole it can be
said that the economic record of the First Republic was a solid
achievement.

In fact, even given the continuing disparities between the
western and eastern regions of the republic, Czechoslovakia
was one of the most highly industrialized and economically

advanced states in interwar Europe—the fifth greatest industrial power on the continent, by some estimates. The proportion of the population engaged in industry, commerce, banking, and transportation—the more "modern" sectors of the economy— was greater in Czechoslovakia than in France, for example. Per capita income was comparatively high. Export goods were known to be of dependable quality, and from railroad cars to the renowned Bat'a shoes, Czechoslovak products competed well in the European markets.

One of the most difficult problems of the interwar economy was the inequality of the First Republic's regions. The free market favored greater development in the already more productive Czech lands. Slovakia was disadvantaged by the fact that its main communication links had grown up with Hungary, from whence most of its prewar capital had come, and connections with the Czech lands were poorly developed. High illiteracy rates characterized both Slovakia and, especially, Ruthenia, and the strength of traditional cultures also contributed to the difficulties of modernization. Czech investors did not generally find the eastern territories favorable ground, and government economists knew little about the economics of underdeveloped regions. Slovakia and Ruthenia benefited from the expansion of the Czech economy: transportation and communications, social and medical services, and education did advance significantly. However, the overall reality was one of economic stagnation in the eastern regions: with 28 percent of Czechoslovakia's total population, Slovakia and Ruthenia produced only 15–18 percent of the national product.

Again, the years of war (1938–45) upset the economic patterns. Although the war inflicted less physical damage on Czechoslovakia than on most other European countries, the economic consequences were not minor. The Protectorate of Bohemia and Moravia was turned into an important source of input for the German war machine, emphasizing the production of coal, steel, and armaments. As a less-developed region and an administratively separate state, Slovakia did not suffer quite so much from planned wartime dislocation; however, there was some substantial physical destruction caused by the protracted struggle of the Slovak resistance. The Third Republic therefore faced serious problems of reconstruction as well as the re-integration of the Czech and Slovak economies.

According to the terms of the Košice Program of April 1945, the postwar economic system was radically changed. For the first time, the state was given a central role in planning, and a big step toward socialist ownership was taken with the nationalization of key industries, banking, insurance, energy, and natural resources. Approximately one-half of the total economic product in 1945–46 came from these state-owned sectors and the other half from private producers and services. Thus the Third Republic was a truly mixed system, part socialist and part private. Properties owned by Sudeten Germans and collaborators were confiscated; industrial properties came under state control, whereas farmlands were divided among private Czech and Slovak farmers. The agricultural system was the subject of a reform in 1947 that left farmlands in private hands but broke up large landholdings, thereby carrying the progressive land reform policies of the interwar period one step further.

A two-year plan was adopted by the government in 1946. The objectives of the plan were very ambitious: complete recovery of the net industrial output to meet and surpass the levels of 1937, similar gains in agriculture, and some reduction of the gap between Slovakia and the Czech lands. Unlike the plans that were to follow the Communist takeover, the 1946 plan left many details to the managers of both private and state-owned enterprises, giving the Third Republic's planning mechanism the loose character of an indicative system of planning, comparable to that of France. Because political events in 1948 disturbed the functioning of the planning apparatus, it is difficult to evaluate the success of the two-year plan. However, the system functioned reasonably well given the unstable circumstances. If plan targets were not fulfilled, at least they served to focus producers' attention on the goals of reconstruction, and by 1948 Czechoslovakia was on the way to recovery from the economic effects of the war.

The Communists therefore inherited a situation in which a part of their work had already been done by the coalition government: major steps had been taken toward institutionalizing socialism and state planning, reconstruction had made substantial progress, production levels were climbing back toward prewar levels, and the economy of Slovakia was finally receiving some much-needed attention. The outlook at the beginning of 1948 was, if not unambiguously bright, certainly cause for some optimism.

THE ECONOMY UNDER COMMUNIST RULE

There was an irony in the application of Stalinist economics to Czechoslovakia. In a sense, the Stalinist formula was more appropriate for the industrialization of Slovakia than for the further development of the Czech lands, yet it was the latter that received the lion's share of capital investment in the new order. In fact, Stalinist economics were hardly apt for Bohemia and Moravia. In its origin, Stalinism was a radical—even controversial—strategy for the transformation of backward Russia to a modern, industrial state on the basis of self-sufficiency. Its adoption by all the governments of Communist-ruled Eastern Europe in their early years illustrated the pervasiveness of the Soviet influence, for the Stalinist strategy ignored specific national circumstances and prescribed a doctrinaire approach that was supposedly of universal validity. For a decade or so, the restructuring of Czechoslovakia's economy resulted in greatly increased capital production, but this came at the expense of balanced development; consumer goods, agriculture, and even technological innovation lagged seriously. By the early 1960s, the economy was in need of a major readjustment, as obsolete plants contributed to very low productivity, food and consumer products were constantly in short supply, and the overall growth rate plummeted to a negative figure in 1963. Still, for reasons that were political rather than economic, reforms were slow in coming, and it was not until 1968 that efforts were taken to implement a comprehensive overhaul of the system.

The Impact of Stalinism

The changes introduced by the Communists soon after the "victorious February" of 1948 were to characterize Czechoslovakia's economic structure, in the main, long after Stalin's death. As in the Soviet model, industry was fully absorbed into the state sector. On January 1, 1949, the first five-year plan was launched according to central directives that were now mandatory rather than indicative. Heavy industry was emphasized and ambitious goals were set: a 57 percent average increase in industrial production, 93 percent in metallurgy, and 100 percent in heavy machinery. Two years into the plan, all targets were raised dramatically—heavy industry by 80 percent over the estimates set in 1948. Nearly half a million workers were expected to take new jobs in industry. The second and third five-year plans (1956–60 and 1961–65, respectively) were similarly aimed at building up heavy industry further and, like the first plan, paid relatively little attention to consumer goods and technological innovation. Quantity was stressed over quality, and the government took great pride in the steeply climbing gross production indexes. Nor was Slovakia left entirely out of the picture. Between 1948 and 1959, industrial production in Slovakia rose by 347 percent (compared to 233 percent in the country as a whole). This impressive statistic notwithstanding, Slovakia's growth was not enough to close the gap between itself and the Czech lands quickly. It has been estimated that, as late as the 1960s, the total industrial product of Slovakia was still less than that of the Ostrava region of Moravia.[3]

Important demographic and social changes accompanied this economic revolution. As the first five-year plan had predicted, there was a rapid increase in the number of industrial workers, drawn into the urban areas from the countryside. This had two positive effects. In the first place, the tendency toward overpopulation of the countryside was reduced, thereby easing the problem of rural unemployment. Secondly, the ranks of the proletariat were augmented by the addition of new recruits—a definite plus in the eyes of party leaders, who saw the growing proletariat as a source of support for the new workers' state. A further important change resulted from the elimination of the property-owning class. The basis of private wealth was removed, adding momentum to the state's conscious policies of income leveling. It should be added that even before 1948, Czech society was one of the most egalitarian in the industrialized world; the Communists' policies pushed the

TABLE 4.1
Growth of Industrial Production, 1948-1960
(Index: 1948 = 100)

	1948	1953[a]	1955[b]	1960[c]
Industry, Total	100	193	224	372
Capital Goods	100	219	249	434
Consumer Goods	100	168	197	307
Electricity	100	165	200	325
Hard Coal	100	145	171	246
Lignite	100	146	202	290
Iron Ore	100	158	174	218
Pig Iron	100	169	181	285
Crude Steel	100	167	171	258
Rolled Steel	100	154	168	252
Cement	100	140	174	305

Source: Author's calculations from raw data in Statistická
Ročenka, 1957, 1961.

[a]Final year of first five-year plan.

[b]Second year of interim plan (1954-55).

[c]Final year of second five-year plan.

leveling process still further, but they did not eliminate inequalities altogether.

The Stalinists also abandoned private agriculture, for the most part forcibly collectivizing the farmlands. This was not done immediately, however; Czechoslovakia's collectivization campaign took place far more slowly and was completed later than that of most other East European countries. The process of bringing farmlands into collective organizations continued throughout the 1950s. Despite the relatively slow pace of collectivization, it was an unpopular policy among the farmers, who by and large strongly preferred to work their own lands for their own profit. Moreover, the Stalinist policy of persecuting and liquidating the so-called *kulaks* (wealthy farmers) had the effect of removing from production those farmers who had been the most successful producers. These factors, coupled with the state's lack of attention to investments in agricultural technology, caused perennial problems in the agricultural sector of the economy. Actual production fell far short of plan targets throughout the first three five-year plans, as is shown in Table 4.2, and hardly surpassed the levels of 1930 by the middle of the third plan (1963).

Given the problems in agriculture and the low priority assigned to production of consumer goods, it is understandable that the standard of living did not improve greatly during this time. Real wages rose fairly consistently, but citizens often found that their increased buying power was diminished because of shortages or poor-quality goods. Certain food items, especially meats, were frequently in short supply, and everyday commodities such as clothing and shoes were often of shoddy quality. Worst of all was the housing shortage, particularly in

TABLE 4.2
Production of Agricultural Goods

Commodity	Unit	Average, 1934-38	1948	1953	1960	1965
Wheat	million tons	1.51	1.43	1.56	1.50	1.99
Rye	"	1.58	1.14	0.95	0.90	0.82
Barley	"	1.11	0.90	1.25	1.74	1.40
Oats	"	1.21	0.99	0.87	1.02	0.63
Potatoes	"	9.64	6.07	9.70	5.09	3.68
Sugar Beets	"	4.66	4.29	5.59	8.34	5.66
Corn	"	0.22	0.30	0.43	0.57	0.39
Fruits and Nuts	"	0.47[a]	0.64	0.72	0.83	0.23
Cows	million head	2.38	1.86	2.15	2.05	1.95
Pigs	"	3.14	2.57	4.17	5.96	5.54
Sheep	"	0.46	0.39	0.98	0.65	0.61
Poultry	"	b	13.48	20.79	28.16	27.75
Index of gross agricultural production (1936 = 100)		100	74.8	87.5	103.1	100.8
Index of agricultural production per hectare (1936 = 100)		100	78.3	93.2	109.9	109.9

Source: Statistická Ročenka for 1957, 1961, and 1966.

[a]1934-37 average.

[b]No data available.

the industrial centers where the population was growing rapidly. Residential flats were scarce (a condition that persists today) and waiting lists very long; it was not uncommon for a young married couple to live with one or the other set of parents for as long as ten years before an apartment would be available for them.

These hardships were partially offset by the relatively low prices set for necessities. Food staples such as bread, potatoes, fruit (in season), and beer—a "necessity" as far as most Czechs are concerned!—were quite cheap. Housing was very cheap: in 1958, rent cost the average worker's family 2 percent or less of its income.[4] Adding to the compensation was the cradle-to-grave welfare system, which provided free medical care and assured the worker of a minimal income after retirement. Luxury items, however, were scarce and expensive: one kilogram of coffee might have cost a worker the equivalent of twenty-five hours' wages, a new automobile several years' earnings.

To some extent, the Czech consumer's loss was the Soviet Union's gain. The economic bonds between the two countries took shape even before the Communist coup in Prague. For example, the Soviets assumed control of the Jáchymov uranium mines at the end of the war and controlled several other important enterprises during the early postwar years. The industries were turned back over to Czechoslovak control later, but the Soviets were granted special privileges and first-priority purchase rights. From 1947 on, trade between the two countries accelerated, beginning with large shipments of Soviet raw materials and food to Czechoslovakia in return for industrial products. As the volume of trade increased, this pattern stabilized. By 1958, the Soviet Union was supplying 99 percent of Czechoslovakia's aluminum, 98 percent of its manganese, 90 percent of its nickel, and high proportions of its required amounts of rubber, copper, iron ore, cotton, corn, wheat, and rye. In exchange, the USSR bought large amounts of manufactured goods, absorbing 99 percent of all Czechoslovak exports of chemical plants and equipment, 90 percent of exported ships, 70 percent of exported rolling stock, and substantial amounts of other capital goods. Eighty-eight percent of Soviet automobile imports were from Czechoslovakia, 44 percent of imported shoes, 32 percent of furniture, and 13 percent of clothing.[5] It is quite clear that the enormous investments in heavy industry served the interests of the USSR at the expense of the Czechoslovak consumer, for Czechs and Slovaks were being asked to sacrifice the development of their consumer goods industries not just to build up their own country's capital stock, but to aid Soviet postwar reconstruction as well. Ironically, however, the trade relationship became far more important to Czechoslovakia's economy than it was to the USSR's, for the Soviets depended much less on imports and exports for the working of their overall economy. This put the Soviets into a position of being able to dictate prices and terms of trade to their own advantage.

The basic components of the economic structure remained stable well into the 1960s. Command planning continued to dominate all sectors, state ownership prevailed in all but a small percentage of the productive enterprises, and collective organizations accounted for more than 87 percent of all croplands. Central planning was still guided by the "iron concept"—emphasis on heavy industry—although some attention had been turned to the plight of the consumer. Yet the standard of living rose slowly, and as the third five-year plan progressed, even heavy industry began to run into snags. Productivity rates fell far short of plan targets, and by 1963 no official explanations could deny the fact that Czechoslovakia was suffering from something that was theoretically not supposed to occur in a socialist society: a major recession. As the sixties developed, Slovak Communists voiced dissatisfaction over the persisting failure of Slovakia to catch up with the Czech lands. An intense debate arose that probed into fundamental issues of socialist economics. Out of this debate came a radical plan for a reform of the system as a whole.

The Rise and Fall of the New Economic Model

For several years prior to the economic bust of 1963, several important economists had begun questioning the system of central planning. As the economic situation worsened, their criticisms captured the attention of reform-oriented party leaders. The economists coupled their critique of the existing system with a complex theoretical argument attacking some of the very fundamentals of Stalinism, and they proposed specific and concrete measures that they believed would cure the country's economic illness. Centered in the Institute of Economics of the Czechoslovak Academy of Sciences, the critical school of economics was led by Ota Šik, an articulate ex-Stalinist who had been influenced by Yugoslav and Polish economists as well as the Soviet economic reformer Yevseĭ Liberman. By 1964 the main ideas of the Šik group had taken shape and proposals for change were being seriously discussed within the highest party circles, but it was not until 1966 that the various opinions could be reconciled around a mutually acceptable program. In June of that year, the Thirteenth Party Congress gave its stamp of approval to a detailed plan that came to be called the New Economic Model, or NEM.

The purpose of the NEM, in its most essential feature, was to get the economy going again. This was to be done by means of a thoroughly revamped system of planning, which the economists argued would be more in tune with the specific conditions of Czechoslovakia in the advanced stage of socialism. By implication, the Stalinist system was a relic of the earlier stage of socialist economic mobilization, and the NEM was clearly meant not to update Stalinism but to replace it.

Briefly put, the NEM called for greatly limiting the role of the central planning authorities. They would no longer plan every detail of production, allocation, and distribution; rather, their task would be to set basic targets. Most of the details of how the targets would be met were to be worked out by middle- and lower-level planners, with the most important responsibility devolving to enterprise managers. Industries would be managed on the basis of profitability, and plant managers would have the authority to determine how the earnings of their plants were to be used—for investment, modernization, expansion, or wage bonuses. Wages and income scales were to be "de-leveled"— that is, keyed more to workers' skills, education, and training— and higher labor productivity was to be stimulated by bonuses and other forms of material incentive. The NEM further envisioned a return to certain features of the market: supply and demand factors would play an important function in determining prices, in most cases within government-imposed ceilings. The central planners, for their part, would continue to regulate prices of such basic commodities as raw materials, energy, and imported capital goods.[6]

Also envisioned in the plan was a major upgrading of technology. A separate research team in the Academy of Sciences, headed by Radovan Richta, published a startling report in 1966 under the title *Civilization at the Crossroads*. In it, the Richta team contradicted the prevailing optimism of the Party, which saw socialist societies catching up to and eventually surpassing the developed capitalist world. Instead, the Richta report argued that Western technology, aided by a scientific revolution, was helping to increase the economic gap between the capitalist and socialist worlds. Although not all of the report's conclusions were accepted by the Party, the leaders were impressed by it and sought to respond to its call for an energetic program of technological development. To the economists, the implications were that research in the applied sciences needed to be stepped up dramatically; at the same time increased economic ties with the West were desirable in order to obtain access to the latest in scientific and technological knowledge. It was with this very objective in mind that the government moved toward normalizing relations with West Germany in 1967—a move that was aborted because of Soviet disapproval.

Conservative forces in the Party recognized that the Šik reforms would have domestic political repercussions, too, and they resisted the new program as long as they could. President Novotný himself had strong misgivings about delegating so much authority to so many managers and technocrats, and he approved the NEM only insofar as the new system left the Party's central policymaking authority intact. The resistance of Novotný and others in command seriously diminished the impact of the NEM during the twelve months following its inauguration in January 1967. As a result, the half-measures that were implemented failed to improve the economy, and by mid-1967 another crisis was unfolding. The seriousness of the economic situation undermined Novotný's position and became one of the most important reasons for his downfall.

Complete implementation of the economic reforms was therefore left to the Dubček regime. Ota Šik, who rose to the position of deputy prime minister in the reform government, forcefully argued the need to follow the New Economic Model in its literal form and without obstructions to its implications. In April, the Party's action program endorsed the plan once again and pledged to implement it fully. In the course of 1968, however, it became clear that there was still no unanimity on many issues in what proved to be a complex debate. Slovak economists, for example, were divided on the question of how much authority to give central planners as opposed to those in the proposed national republics; thus the economic program got mixed up with the discussion of federalism, as many influential Slovaks questioned the wisdom of a uniform policy for both halves of the country. Trade union leaders worried that profitability considerations might lead to the shutdown of inefficient plants, threatening unemployment or dislocation for many workers. Despite the fact that there was a strong consensus in favor of meaningful reforms along the lines of the NEM, the Party and government were unable to work out all the complexities of the economic problem by the time of the invasion. The main opposition to the general program had been defeated, though, and the discussions were moving forward.

A further issue entered the debate during the Prague Spring, giving an added political overtone to the economic question. This concerned what was variously called "enterprise democracy," the "democratic organization of management," "factory councils," and other similar terms. The idea, associated with Šik and also Zdeněk Mlynář, was reminiscent of Yugoslav workers' councils. Again, varying forms of the idea were batted about, though all of them presumed some degree of comanagement between workers and plant directors. The government gave its approval to the formation of councils in June, and the trade unions agreed. Even though the details of their organization, functions, selection, and legal status were not decided, workers' councils began to form in many factories. The councils were to consult with and advise the industrial management in the running of their plants. They would be democratically elected by the workers from among their own ranks, and they would represent the interests of their constituencies in the making of important production decisions. Councils continued to form even after the occupation of Czechoslovakia, in defiance of Soviet wishes to the contrary. Their formation reflected a high level of interest among the workers and lent the economic reform movement an air of real democracy.

As with most other reforms, the NEM was stillborn. In limbo between the invasion and the removal of Dubček, the NEM came increasingly under attack by Party spokesmen. By the end of 1969, it was totally abandoned as a "romantic notion" (in Husák's words), along with all thoughts of workers' councils. Šik, who went into exile, was personally condemned and his theories discredited; all who had worked with him were similarly disgraced. Economic planning was returned to the central state planning apparatus, and decentralization became a concept officially associated with negative memories, never to be revived. Although managers seem to have greater influence since 1968 than they did before the experiment with the NEM, their authority is much less than that of the state planners. Market forces are not important in pricing decisions, and resource allocation is again determined by government decisions.

Nor has federalism significantly diminished the centralized nature of the post-1968 system. Originally, a considerable degree of economic autonomy was envisioned for the two halves of the republic, but the tendency toward political recentralization in the 1970s carried over into economic organization as well. Tasks that were assigned earlier to the national republics were taken over gradually by the federal government, and the integrated character of the Czechoslovak economic system is now given emphasis. As in political affairs, economic organization thus centers in Prague, the seat of most decision-making authority.

INTO THE FUTURE

With the New Economic Model only a discomfiting memory, the regime has moved toward the promising future of developed socialism—a higher stage of social advancement that the Party, sensitive to questions of political reform, prefers to describe primarily in economic terms. Thanks to some modest reforms in the economic structure and to Soviet loans of hard currency, the regime has been able to provide the citizens with an improving standard of living. By the late 1970s, nonetheless, the economy had begun to show trouble signs once again, and the government struggled to control the many uncertainties of the situation.

Economic Development in the 1970s

The Husák regime has obviously put great store in the development of the economy. On the one hand, the Party and government in the post-1968 years have desperately wanted to prove the correctness of their hard line in both political and economic affairs, and on the other, they have unabashedly sought to woo public support—or at least quiescence—by raising the standard of living. To improve the functioning of the economy, the government enacted a conservative reform along the lines of Soviet organizational reforms of the 1970s. Within the centralized planning structure, a three-tier system of management has emerged, featuring a middle layer of managers between the central planners at the top and the plant managers below. The middle tier is organized in production-economic units, analogous to cartels and similar in concept to those first adopted in East Germany during the 1960s. The managers of the middle tier have wide-ranging responsibilities in administering the details of the central plan within their respective units, but they are subordinate to the top economic planners.

Ironically, the organizational reform has so far had little effect on overall economic performance. The economy had improved in the early 1970s, thanks to vigorous investment efforts and a substantial dose of Soviet aid. By 1975, when the reform first came into effect, problems had begun to appear in several sectors, and since then the difficulties have multiplied.

In overall terms, the economy moved along reasonably well throughout the decade. Plans were for the most part fulfilled, and growth took place at a satisfactory rate. As late as 1979, government leaders expressed satisfaction with the achievement of growth rates commensurate with the goals of the sixth five-year plan (1976–80). Consumer goods have become more available, helped along by increased imports of such items as clothing and electronic gadgets from the West, and the standard of living has risen measurably. Especially noteworthy is the success in the industrialization of Slovakia; to be sure, there remain many rural pockets of backwardness and poverty in the Slovak hinterlands, but in gross industrial production the Slovak republic has nearly caught up with the Czech republic. One can see the results as one travels through the developed areas of Slovakia and encounters many bustling industrial centers that were sleepy towns not long ago.

Under the surface, however, problems have been brewing. These became apparent late in 1974 as high levels of investment failed to yield commensurate output, indicating a slackening in productivity. Personal consumption had risen consistently up to that point, but thereafter its rate of increase slowed down. Inflationary tendencies in the world market caught up with the Czechoslovak economy, forcing the government to adjust some prices upward, thereby disturbing the price stability the government had worked hard to establish. In the second half of the decade, more and more problems emerged, directing planners' attention to serious disorders with long-term implications. Meat shortages began to occur in 1978, and agricultural production in general failed to reach the production goals set in the five-year plan. The winter of 1978–79 saw power outages and shortages of heating fuel. Poor-quality industrial goods and continuing low productivity rates prompted the adoption of an experimental program, adopted in 1978 for testing at some 150 plants, aimed at ensuring greater efficiency and improved workmanship. Yet it was obvious that underlying these visible problems was the fact that much of the industrial plant and equipment was obsolete or obsolescent—perhaps as much as 70 percent by some estimates.

Still more serious was the realization that energy shortages were looming on the horizon. The world oil crisis was having its effect on the socialist community, as the Soviet Union simultaneously reduced its production and raised its prices. In the middle of 1979, the government announced that the price of home heating oil would go up by 125 percent—from 68 cents to $1.54 per gallon. With consumption of electrical energy threatening to exceed supply, the cost of electricity went up by 50 percent, as did that of coal. Toward the end of the decade, the government, faced with the certainty of future energy shortfalls, found itself impelled toward the prospect of increasing reliance on nuclear power.

The first atomic power plant, located at Jaslovské Bohunice in Slovakia, began operations on a trial basis in December 1978. Throughout 1979, there were reports of problems in the plant, including unconfirmed rumors that two accidents, at least one of them fatal, had occurred.[7] The government nevertheless pressed ahead with plans to open further nuclear power stations at Dukovany in the early 1980s and Mochovice in the mid-1980s. Time will tell whether or not nuclear power can solve Czechoslovakia's energy problems. The prospect is of course very expensive, and Soviet aid will be crucial. Whether or not the Soviets will provide enough help—and whether or not Czechoslovakia can afford a large-scale program of nuclear energy development—is still a question.

All of Czechoslovakia's economic problems as of the late 1970s seemed to require outside help. In the course of the decade, the Soviets had shown an increasing reluctance to bail their East European allies out of what was becoming a growing economic morass. To be sure, one could assume that the Soviets would not let Czechoslovakia or any other CMEA member sink into oblivion, but at the same time they were letting it be known that they would not pay an unlimited bill in order to subsidize East European prosperity. Czechoslovakia's leaders therefore began to look cautiously westward for much-needed technological assistance. From 1977 on, slow progress was made in obtaining credits, attracting Western firms to embark on construction projects in Czechoslovakia, and exploring the possibilities of technology transfer. These efforts were hampered by

an already unfavorable balance of trade, and government officials remained unsure about what to do. Early in 1978, for
example, the hope was expressed that $3 billion worth of ad-
vanced equipment and technology could be purchased from the
West by 1980; the following year, a worsened trade deficit forced
the government to think a second time about increasing the
level of foreign debt.

The consumer was faced with an equally uncertain future.
Higher prices were eating into his standard of living, and frequent "meatless Mondays" were constraining his dietary habits.
He had become accustomed to the family automobile, the
vacation cottage, and certain items of Western-made clothing;
could his budget absorb what were sure to be continued price
increases without depressing his lifestyle? Perhaps more serious
was the question of supply: could the economy continue to
provide consumer goods and at the same time redress the
basic problems of technology and energy supply? Already the
black market, that long-familiar facet of socialist society that
seems to survive all other twists and turns of economic reality,
was reaching record proportions. No one knows just how large
a role the "second economy" plays in socialist countries, at
least not in precisely quantifiable figures, but it flourished in
the 1970s as never before.

A word about this peculiar phenomenon is in order. The
black market thrives wherever legal economic practices fail to
distribute available goods and services to all who are able and
willing to pay for them. "Available" in this sense has a relative
meaning; those who illegally purvey the goods or services in
demand know that what they have to sell is either unavailable
through the legitimate channels or not available in sufficient
quantities to satisfy demand. The black market therefore acts
as a kind of regulator, satisfying certain consumer demands at
generally very high prices, which the buyer is willing to pay
simply because he cannot otherwise get the product or service.
Any Westerner who has visited Czechoslovakia is likely to have
been approached and offered very favorable rates of currency
exchange by private citizens who desire Western cash, either for
a planned trip abroad or to spend in the government's "dollar
shops" on luxury items unobtainable in normal shops. Many

kinds of consumer goods produced in the West, from pocket
calculators to Volkswagen parts, will bring inflated prices on the
black market. Building materials and other goods, pilfered from
state enterprise supplies, can often be had if the price is right.
Services that are in short supply—car repair, plumbing, electrical
work, and so on—may not be available through the certified
agencies for months, but a workman can usually be found who
will perform the service on his off hours for several times the
officially approved cost. Often, one service is exchanged for another: if X, an auto mechanic, will tune the engine of Y's Škoda,
then Y, a plumber, will unclog X's drain and fix his leaky toilet.
Bribery is a common feature of the "second economy," and
officially frowned-upon "tips" will usually assure a person of
better service, be it in fuel delivery or the delivery of a baby,
than will paying only the government-approved charges. In contemporary Czechoslovakia these illegal economic activities are
pervasive features of everyday life. Practiced even by Party
members and government officials, they are symptomatic of an
economic system that, despite its positive accomplishments, has
not fulfilled the expectations of the consumers.

Toward Developed Socialism?

As Czechoslovakia moves toward a new phase in its social
evolution, theory predicts that economic difficulties will be
overcome. This is not to say that there will be no contradictions
in the process of advancing into the stage of developed socialism,
but rather that, with enlightened political leadership, the dialectical logic of history will prevail over the contradictions.
Party theorists have predicted that Czechoslovakia will be a
developed socialist society within the next two decades, so the
overriding task is to prepare for a timely entry into the new
phase.

Despite the fact that the Soviet Union has already entered
the stage, theorists have not yet defined the characteristics of
developed socialism very clearly. It is said to be defined by ma-
turity of productive forces and characterized by a high standard
of labor productivity and by the predominance of large and
technologically advanced cooperative enterprises. It also features
maximally effective management methods and a well-rounded

pattern of growth sufficient to guarantee future production, provide secure military defenses, and offer every citizen a comfortable standard of living. In the political sphere, developed socialism embodies efforts to perfect the institutions of socialist democracy and draw all workers into a participatory role. In some socialist countries, notably Poland and Hungary, there is evidence that the development of socialist democracy is taken quite seriously, as the government is trying to broaden decision making in the factories and encourage public participation in local government.

For reasons having to do with the negative memory of 1968, the Czechoslovak leadership is unwilling to take meaningful steps toward socialist democracy and prefers, instead, to view developed socialism in strictly economic terms. Thus the task entails rectifying the current disorders in the economy and putting it on a firm basis for the long-range future. As we have seen, that is already proving to be a complicated assignment. Many of the structural deficiencies that came to the fore in the 1960s have not been overcome. Patchwork reforms, Soviet subsidies, and the exhortatory banners and slogans one sees in and around factories are obviously not enough to propel Czechoslovakia along toward the promising threshold of developed socialism. As the 1970s drew to a close, the Party and government found themselves in an unprecedentedly complex situation, leading a society with high consumer expectations, confronting a political opposition whose voice can be clearly heard by a potentially responsive populace that has so far been kept quiet with material palliatives, and faced with awesome decisions whose effects could very well destabilize the political status quo.

NOTES

1. R. H. Osborne, *East-Central Europe: An Introductory Geography* (New York: Praeger Publishers, 1967), p. 129.

2. Zora P. Pryor, "Czechoslovak Economic Devleopment in the Inter-war Period," in Victor S. Mamatey and Radomír Luža, eds., *A History*

of the Czechoslovak Republic 1918–1948 (Princeton, N.J.: Princeton University Press, 1973), p. 190.

3. Otto Ulč, *Politics in Czechoslovakia* (San Francisco: W. H. Freeman and Co., 1974), p. 49.

4. Edward A. Taborsky, *Communism in Czechoslovakia 1948–1960* (Princeton, N.J.: Princeton University Press, 1961), p. 437.

5. Zdenek Suda, *The Czechoslovak Socialist Republic* (Baltimore, Md.: Johns Hopkins University Press, 1969), pp. 55–57.

6. The Czechoslovak reforms were similar to plans simultaneously developed by Hungarian economists. The Hungarian New Economic Mechanism, as it is called, went into effect in 1968 and has since undergone some modifications. On the whole, it has been rather successful.

7. Charter 77 published a document reporting the two accidents, but the regime refused to admit that the accidents had occurred.

5

Czechoslovak Society

One's first impression of Czechoslovak society might be that it is rather uncomplicated, since the population is small and the pressures of political conformity are great. In fact, the society is quite complex. Some of its complexities stem from the specific histories of its various regions and peoples, whereas others are the result of general social forces common to all modern societies. This chapter will survey Czechoslovak society, looking first at its ethnic and nationality make-up, then at its religious groupings, and finally at its social structure.[1]

ETHNIC AND NATIONAL GROUPS

The world of the twentieth century is composed of many states with varied patterns of ethnic and national populations, and there are few better examples of this than Czechoslovakia. When the country was founded in 1918, it was named for the two major Slavic communities that inhabited most of its territory. At the same time, large minority populations also found themselves within the borders of the new state. As we have seen in Chapter 1, conflicts among these groups contributed to the destruction of the First Republic by providing an entrée for Hitler, who shrewdly used Czechoslovakia's ethnic strife in applying his divide-and-rule tactics. After 1945 the problem of the minorities subsided, and the distrust between Czechs and Slovaks was swept beneath the surface of Communist rule. Yet Slovak nationalism, which had been such a destructive force in the late 1930s, reemerged in a different form during the

1960s as Slovak Communists rose to positions of power and led the movement for a federal system. Today, nationality conflicts are perhaps not as sharp as they have been, but in subtle ways they continue to be expressed.

Czechs and Slovaks generally perceive themselves as separate nations, with their own distinct languages and cultural traditions. This two-nations view was a matter of serious controversy during the time of the First Republic, when the dominant assumption among the political elite held that there was only one "Czechoslovak" nation—a premise that underlay much of the earlier movement toward the foundation of the Czechoslovak republic.[2] The "Czechoslovak" idea was disputed by many people, including the Slovak nationalists (especially the Hlinka group) and an important faction in the Communist Party. The grievances of the Slovak nationalists led them into collaboration with Hitler, and, as a result of the fratricidal conflict between Czechs and Slovaks, the Czechoslovak idea became discredited and was abandoned by the end of the Second World War. Since 1945 the government has officially acknowledged the national distinctness of Czechs and Slovaks, and in 1968–69 the adoption of a federal system gave institutional substance to the two-nations assumption.

Ethnic minorities are recognized and accorded certain group rights (see discussion p. 129ff). They do not have effective political representation as corporate groups, however, and therefore they frequently feel themselves to be second-class citizens whose ethnic rights are entirely subject to the will of the dominant Czechs and Slovaks. The largest minority today are the Hungarians, but even they do not represent a great proportion of the total population. Nonetheless, their collective self-perception as second-class citizens poses a problem of some sensitivity.

Czechs and Slovaks

Together, Czechs and Slovaks comprise more than 94 percent of Czechoslovakia's population, with Czechs outnumbering Slovaks by approximately two to one (see Table 5.1). The boundaries of the Czech and Slovak republics do not correspond perfectly to ethnic settlement patterns, for there are

TABLE 5.1
Czechoslovakia's Population According to Nationality, 1930 and 1977

Nationality	Population (Thousands) 1930	Population (Thousands) 1977[a]	Percent of Total 1930	Percent of Total 1977[a]
Czechs	} 9,689	9,655	} 66.9	64.0
Slovaks		4,563		30.3
Germans	3,232	77	22.3	0.5
Hungarians	692	600	4.8	4.0
Ukrainians	549	51	3.8	0.3
Poles	82	78	0.6	0.5
Others and Unknown[b]	236	58	1.6	0.4
Total	14,480	15,082	100.0	100.0

Source: Statistická Ročenka Republiky Československé 1935 (Prague) and Statistická Ročenka ČSSR 1978 (Prague).

[a]Estimated population as of December 1977.

[b]Includes Jews who declare themselves as such, as well as Russians, Gypsies, Romanians, and Yugoslavs.

many Czechs living in Slovakia and many Slovaks in the Czech lands. Patterns of migration caused a mixing of the two groups even before 1918, particularly in eastern Moravia and western Slovakia. The father of Tomáš Masaryk, for example, was a Slovak who had migrated across the old border and married a Moravian woman.

During the time of the First Republic many Czechs moved to Slovakia, where a shortage of teachers, administrators, other professionals, and skilled workers offered the promise of economic advancement and the challenge of opening up new markets, schools, offices, and factories. The end of Austro-Hungarian rule resulted in capital flight, and Slovakia in particular became open territory for Czech financial interests. At first, it was obvious that Czechs were needed to fill in the professional gaps; later, however, many Slovaks came to resent what they saw as the "colonization" of their land by the Czechs, especially when the depression threw many people out of work. Slovak nationalists made an issue out of "Czech colonialism," accusing the Czechs of a deliberate attempt to undermine national solidarity among the Slovaks.

Since the Second World War there has been some movement of Slovaks to the Czech lands, but this has by no means become an overwhelming trend. As Table 5.2 shows, Czechs are still by far the dominant group in the Czech republic, as are Slovaks in Slovakia.

In the past few decades, a higher birth rate among Slovaks has increased their population relative to that of the Czechs, but the Czechs remain a majority in the country as a whole (see Table 5.3). The Slovaks' higher birth rate reflects the continuing strength of traditional values that are not as compelling to Czechs: a desire to have large families, religious beliefs that discourage birth control, and conservative attitudes about the role of women in society. Future trends are never easy to predict, but there is reason to believe that the increasing modernization of Slovakia will weaken the pull of these traditional orientations and cause the birth rate to level off. Czechs, therefore, will probably maintain their numerical preponderance for an indefinite time.

There has always been some ambivalence in the Czechs' and Slovaks' attitudes toward each other. Czechs have traditionally viewed Slovaks as their close ethnic relatives, possess-

TABLE 5.2
Nationality Population in Each Republic, 1977

| Nationality | Czech Lands | | Slovakia | |
	Thousands	Percent	Thousands	Percent
Czechs	9,604	94.0	51	1.0
Slovaks	387	3.8	4,176	85.8
Germans	73	0.7	4	< 0.1
Hungarians	22	0.2	578	11.9
Ukrainians	10	< 0.1	41	0.8
Poles	76	0.7	3	< 0.1
Others and Unknown	44	0.4	14	0.3

Source: Statistická Ročenka ČSSR 1978 (Prague).

ing similar physical traits but socially more primitive. The Czech image of the Slovak as a "younger brother," popular at the turn of the century, colored Czech attitudes for a long time and gave the relationship a benign but definite air of condescension. The Czechoslovak movement was not immune to such feelings; while Masaryk and many others genuinely believed in the national unity of the two peoples and strove to give them equal positions in the Czechoslovak partnership, others—including some Slovaks—considered the Slovaks backward and in need of tutelage. To this day one can find similar sentiments among many Czechs. Despite the modernization of Slovakia, Slovaks as a people are often pictured by Czechs as unsophisticated, not highly cultured, and oriented toward traditional, provincial modes and lifestyles.

The resentment of Slovaks toward Czechs that built up between the two world wars was perpetuated after 1948, for the Communist regime was strongly dominated by Czechs who cared nothing about Slovak national aspirations. Despite the government's official acknowledgment of the two-nations

TABLE 5.3
Ratio of Slovaks to Czechs[a] in Bohemia, Moravia, and Slovakia, 1930-1977

Nationality	1930[b]	1950	1960	1977[c]
Czechs	100.0	100.0	100.0	100.0
Slovaks	30.9	38.7	42.3	47.3

Source: Calculated by the author according to raw data taken from Statistická Ročenka for 1961 and 1978.

[a]Statistics are given as a ratio in which the Czech population is given the constant index of 100.

[b]The 1930 census data did not precisely distinguish between Czechs and Slovaks; the raw data on which the 1930 ratios are based are official estimates made after 1945.

[c]Based on estimates of the population as of December 1977.

principle, the Communists ruled through a highly centralized power structure. During the Stalin period, those who dared to identify themselves with Slovak nationalism were considered criminals, and several of the leading Slovak Communists were convicted of supposed crimes linked to "bourgeois nationalism"; among them were Gustáv Husák, now the president of the republic, the poet Laco Novomeský, and Vlado Clementis, a prominent Slovak Communist who was executed for his alleged crimes. Given this background, the Slovaks' struggle in the 1960s for a federal system represented a courageous stand that persevered in the face of great obstacles.

The federalization reform of 1968, therefore, has an importance that transcends the specific structural features of the new political system and even, to some extent, counterbalances the shortcomings of the reform in practice. It represents a turning point in Czech-Slovak relations, heralding the end of the lengthy controversy over unitary rule versus federalism and Prague centralism versus some form of autonomy for Slovakia. Interestingly, during the 1970s Slovaks occupied many visible positions of authority in Prague, including not only Husák's dual position as president and Party chief but also the key ministries of foreign affairs (Bohuš Chňoupek), defense (Martin Dzúr), and foreign trade (Andrej Barčák).[3] By thus achieving a measure of political power beyond their proportion of the country's total population, Slovaks have aroused some resentment among Czechs, who now perceive a reversal in the pattern of national dominance.

National tensions between Czechs and Slovaks are nothing new; they have been apparent ever since independence. Although these tensions are important and must be understood as a reality of life in modern Czechoslovakia, they should not be allowed to blot out our awareness of the factors serving to unite Czechs and Slovaks. The two peoples have been joined together politically for most of the twentieth century. Their societies, while distinct in many respects, have taken on a number of common features as a result of their close interaction over the course of two and one-half generations. Their languages, Czech and Slovak, are so closely related that they are mutually and easily understandable, and therefore communication between the two groups has always flowed smoothly. Modern highways, radio, and television have brought Czechs and Slovaks together daily, penetrating into the most remote mountain villages. If national resentments continue to exist, they are at the same time counterbalanced by stronger mutual resentments toward the traditional enemies—Germans, Hungarians, Poles—and, since 1968, the Russians. The assumption and adoption of a federal system by the two nations have not weakened the ties between Czechs and Slovaks; in the long run the country may find itself stronger, and its two dominant national groups more deeply bound together, by the official acknowledgment that they are separate but equal.

Ethnic Minorities

A glance at Table 5.1 (p. 125) will reveal that the ethnic composition of Czechoslovakia has changed dramatically since 1930. The First Republic was a crazy quilt of ethnic groups, and only if Czechs and Slovaks were counted together could an ethnic majority be identified within a society that included substantial numbers of Germans, Hungarians, Ukrainians, Jews, Poles, and Gypsies. Today, in contrast, Czechs and Slovaks account for all but 5.7 percent of the population, and Czechs themselves comprise a majority.

The changes that brought about this ethnic restructuring originated during World War II. First there came the decimation of Czechoslovakia's Jewish community—a familiar and tragic story. As a result of genocide, deportations, and emigration between 1938 and 1945, the number of Jews in Czechoslovakia declined by nearly 80 percent. Table 5.4 shows this decline in Bohemia, Moravia, and Slovakia. There were, in addition, some 102,000 Jews living in Subcarpathian Ruthenia, of whom it is presumed that few survived the Nazi genocidal terror.

By the end of the war Czechoslovakia had also lost most of its Ukrainian minority, as the eastern territory of Ruthenia was ceded to the USSR. Still more dramatic was the disappearance of the Sudeten Germans. Between 1945 and 1950, about 95 percent of the large German minority was forced to leave Czechoslovakia under the terms of the expulsion law. Finally,

TABLE 5.4
Effect of the Holocaust: Czechoslovakia's Jewish Population, 1930-1945

Region	1930 Census	1945 Estimate	Change
Bohemia and Moravia	117,551	22,000	-95,551
Slovakia	136,737	31,500	-105,237
Total, Czechoslovakia (excluding Ruthenia)	254,288	53,500	-200,788

Source: Ludvík Němec, "Solution of the Minorities Problem," in Victor
S. Mamatey and Radomír Luža, eds., A History of the Czechoslovak Republic 1918-1948 (Princeton, N.J.: Princeton University Press, 1973), pp.
425-26.

approximately 150,000 Hungarians left between 1945 and 1948 as the result of a policy of partial expulsion. Only about 20 percent of the Hungarian minority had fled by the time the policy was abandoned in the interest of harmony between the Prague and Budapest governments.

The Polish minority remained about the same size after the war as it had been before 1938, but not before some shifting took place in the meantime. Large numbers of Poles inhabited several districts of northern Slovakia that were seized by Poland in 1938. As a result of the German-Soviet occupation of Poland in 1939, these territories and their inhabitants were given over to the wartime Slovak state, and they passed back to Czechoslovakia in 1945.

Today, Hungarians constitute the largest minority (not counting the Slovaks, who are constitutionally described as a "nation" rather than as an ethnic minority). Amounting to only 4 percent of the total population, the Hungarians are a marginal group in Czechoslovak society. Nonetheless, it is worth noting that they are not, by and large, well assimilated into the mainstream. As a group, they tend to be less well educated than Czechs and Slovaks. Proportionally fewer of them are able to pursue careers in the professions, and they tend to be underrepresented in the state's political institutions. They are allowed to develop their own cultural institutions, for which the state puts out a financial subsidy, and their children are in many instances able to attend schools in which the Hungarian language is the primary medium of instruction. At the same time, a fluent knowledge of Slovak or Czech is a prerequisite for a university education, and those whose command of the dominant language is imperfect find themselves disadvantaged when taking the entrance exams.

On occasion, voices of discontent have been heard among Czechoslovakia's Hungarians. In 1968, for example, some Hungarians openly called for a change in their status that would give them and other minorities the same constitutional rights accorded to Czechs and Slovaks, including corporate representation in the political system. Interestingly, the vehicle through which the Hungarian demands were issued was Csemadok, the officially created organization set up to give the Hungarians a controlled representation within the National Front. The demands of Csemadok were not taken up by the reformers of 1968, because the Slovak leaders feared that Hungarian power within a federalized state would weaken Slovakia, as most of the Hungarian minority live in Slovakia.

Since 1968, Csemadok has been "normalized"; that is to say, its leadership has been purged and the organization brought once again under the regime's control. Like other problems in contemporary Czechoslovakia, the Hungarians' discontent has been swept under the rug. Whether or not this particular problem will ever be of great importance to Czechoslovak politics is hard to say; the Hungarians comprise only a minor part of the country's total population (although they are almost 12 percent of the population of Slovakia). On the other hand, the worsening political conditions of the 1970s served to alienate the Hungarian minority more than ever and focused their loyalties on the country to the south—Kádár's Hungary—where their ethnic kinfolk were enjoying a more relaxed political atmosphere and a cultural flowering. Thus the status of Czechoslovakia's disaffected Hungarian minority, living mostly in southern Slovakia toward the border with Hungary, is a sensitive issue in the two countries' relations and represents a sore spot in the Communist bloc.

Another sore spot in bloc relations has centered around

Czechoslovakia's small Ukrainian minority. These people, living mostly in the easternmost districts of Slovakia, have long been divided on the exact nature of their national identity. Their language is a dialect of Ukrainian and their ethnic ancestry is the same as that of today's Soviet Ukrainians; however, they share a common history not with the majority of Soviet Ukrainians but rather with those living in the smallish province of Subcarpathian Ruthenia, annexed by the Soviet Union in 1945. Many of them prefer to emphasize their ethnic distinctiveness by referring to themselves as Ruthenians (*Rusyny*), thereby expressing a nationalistic identity that reaches across the Czechoslovak-Soviet border. Within the Soviet Ukraine, the "Ruthenian question" causes problems of divided loyalties. In deference to Soviet wishes, the official policy of the Czechoslovak state has always been to encourage its own segment of this community to identify themselves as "Ukrainians" and thereby undercut the solidarity of Ruthenian nationalism.

In 1968, a number of Czechoslovak Ukrainians began to agitate on behalf of Ruthenian nationalism, demanding minority rights within Czechoslovakia similar to those sought by the Hungarians. News of their activities was regularly broadcast by a Ukrainian-language radio station in Prešov and picked up by radios in the western Ukraine. The subversive impact of these broadcasts was perhaps exaggerated by the Soviet leadership, but it is clear that concern over the situation was one factor in the growing Soviet hostility to the Dubček government. The Ruthenian demands, like those of the Hungarian minority, were not taken very seriously by the reformers in Prague and were strongly denounced by most of the Slovak leaders, but the official disapproval did not lessen the international tension generated by the movement.

The remaining minority groups—Germans, Poles, Jews, and Gypsies—have been relatively quiescent throughout the postwar period. In 1968 spokesmen for the Germans, Poles, and Gypsies came forward with modest programs of minority rights for their respective communities, but again, these proposals did not become official policy, and the smallness of the groups made them no threat to the regime.

Minority relations in Czechoslovakia hardly present a problem as critical as that faced by the First Republic in the 1930s. On the other hand, the lingering resentments underlying the surface of society demonstrate that the Communists have been unable to assimilate the minorities. This should not be surprising in light of the widespread rise of ethnic politics in the twentieth-century world. It does suggest that Communist regimes, despite their frequent claims to the contrary, have not discovered the solution to problems of ethnic and national conflict. According to Marxist-Leninist theory, such conflict was presumed to be integrally connected with bourgeois notions of political loyalty and therefore was theoretically destined to disappear along with other social evils of the capitalist era. Instead, it lives on.

RELIGION

It is difficult to assemble accurate statistics about church membership in Czechoslovakia, but one estimate has it that approximately 70 percent of the population are Roman Catholics, 15 percent are Protestants, and the remaining 15 percent have no religious affiliation.[4] Roman Catholicism is by far the most prevalent religion in both halves of the country. In Slovakia there are significant numbers of Orthodox and Greek Catholics, numbering several hundred thousand together. (The Greek Catholic, or Uniate, Church observes the Orthodox liturgy but recognizes the authority of the Roman Pope.) The Judaic religious community is estimated at around 16,000. All in all, nineteen religious denominations are officially recognized (see Table 5.5), though many of them can claim only very small memberships.

The composition of the Protestant groups varies in the two republics. In Slovakia, the Evangelical (Lutheran) Church is the largest Protestant sect, although among the Hungarian minority the Reformed (Calvinist) Church is larger. In the Czech Republic, the Czechoslovak Church is the largest Protestant denomination, although it is perhaps rivaled in some regions of Moravia by the Evangelical Church. Several branches of

TABLE 5.5
Religious Denominations Accorded Legal Status in Czechoslovakia

Roman Catholic Church	Council of Jewish Religious
Old Catholic Church	Communities in the Czech Lands
Eastern Orthodox Church	Central Union of Jewish
Greek Catholic (Uniate) Church	Religious Communities in
	Slovakia

Protestant Denominations

Czechoslovak Church*	Religious Society of Czechoslovak
Slovak Evangelical Church	Unitarians
of the Augsburg Confession	Christian Congregations in
Silesian Evangelical Church	Czechoslovakia
of the Augsburg Confession	Unity of Brethren
Slovak Reformed Christian Church	Unity of Czech Brethren
Evangelic Methodist Church	Evangelical Church of Czech Brethren
Brotherly Unity of Baptists	Seventh Day Adventists
	New Apostolic Church

Source: Vladimir V. Kusin, Political Grouping in the Czechoslovak Reform Movement (New York: Columbia University Press, 1972), p. 206.

*Note: The Czechoslovak Church was founded in 1920 by a number of priests who originally sought to liberalize Catholic theology. It eventually grew into a sizable denomination with some 850,000 members by the mid-1930s and took on an increasingly liberal theological orientation as it did so.

the Brethren are also fairly large.

Even taken as crude estimates, the available statistics on church affiliation do not indicate the strength of religious beliefs among the populace or the extent of actual religious practice—both of which vary greatly but are in general fairly low. A small number of sociological studies undertaken between 1962 and 1968 suggested that religiosity tended to be quite widespread in Slovakia but less strong elsewhere. A study of religious attitudes in North Moravia, for example, indicated that only 30 percent of the persons interviewed considered themselves believers, while another 30 percent were atheists and 40 percent undecided. A similar study in Slovakia, however, found that more than 70 percent of the respondents there were believers.[5]

The Religious Heritage

Religious traditions in the two halves of Czechoslovakia are quite different from each other. The Hussite legacy is a valued part of the Czech national heritage, and despite the forced re-Catholicization of Bohemia during the Counter-Reformation, a "protestant" spirit has permeated Czech religious orientations throughout the ages. Under Jesuit control, Czech Catholicism took on a certain national peculiarity, and Bohemia was relatively hospitable ground for liberal Catholic theologies. This was not true of Slovakia, where Roman Catholicism has always retained a strong traditionalist character, and where the popular image of Prague as the center of heresy has long contributed to Slovak suspicions of the Czechs. This image was particularly strong among the followers of Hlinka in the First Republic and reached a fever pitch in the ranks of the World War II Tiso government.

Countering this somewhat artificial religious cleavage between Czechs and Slovaks was the tradition of cooperation and mutual support between the Protestants of the two nations, dating back to the Hussite era. Protestants played disproportionately more important roles in the nineteenth-century "awakenings" of both nations, and Protestants again dominated the ruling group of the First Republic. Palacký, Havlíček, Rieger, Kollár, Šafárik, and Štúr were all Protestants, as were Hodža and, importantly, Masaryk (who converted to Protestantism in part as a means of expressing his identification with the national heritage). Both the Matice česká and the Matica slovenská were dominated by Protestants in their formative years, and the intellectual cooperation that centered around the Czechoslovak Union (a political activist movement) at the turn of the century had a distinctly Protestant tone about it (though some important figures in the movement, such as Pavol Blaho, were Catholics).

This strong background of Protestant intellectual collaboration underlay the entire Czechoslovak movement and, later, served as the basis of Czech-Slovak unity in the First Republic. To some extent, the conflict that developed between the Slovak nationalists and those who upheld the idea of Czechoslovak national unity correlated with religious orientations: Slovak Catholic nationalists versus "Czechoslovak" Protestants.[6]

Religion Under Communist Rule

Marx's dictum that religion is an "opium of the people" and must be eliminated has underlain church-state relations ever since the Communists assumed power. In 1949 the state assumed responsibility for the financial needs of the churches, but in return for giving the churches rather stingy support, the state has demanded that they yield to the state authority over most of their affairs. A commissioner for church affairs holds the rank of minister in the federal government, and a chain of political command leads from this position downward all the way to local secretaries for church affairs. Through this political command system the government watches the activities of the clergy and ensures that they abstain from influencing their congregations in ways that are contrary to the wishes of the Party. Ministers and priests are required to avoid practical social questions in their sermons and are expected to encourage their flock to uphold and support the aims of socialism. The Party endorses a Catholic organization called Pacem in Terris, whose members are priests who have expressed their willingness to actively promote the Party's policies within the church community. Not all priests join Pacem in Terris, but those who do work to ensure that church policies do not challenge the Party's control. Although the Protestant churches are subject to the same strictures of surveillance and control, the Roman and Greek Catholic Churches have come under especially rough treatment because of their connections with a foreign source of authority (the Vatican). Mass arrests of priests took place in 1949; especially severe sentences were handed down to church leaders such as Josef Cardinal Beran (fourteen years' imprisonment, which he served completely), Bishop Štěpan Trochta of Litoměřice (twenty-five years), and Bishops Karel Skoupý of Brno and Josef Hlouč of České Budějovice (twenty years each). Many other priests, monks, and nuns were jailed or forced into menial labor on farms or in factories. Charges leveled against those who were brought to trial were usually treason, espionage, and subversive contacts with the Vatican.

The Greek Catholic Church suffered the same persecutions plus one more: it was outlawed in 1950, as it had been in the USSR three years earlier. Its adherents were required to transfer their loyalties to the Orthodox Church. The reason for this arbitrary policy was connected to the problem of Ruthenian nationalism. Organized mainly in eastern Slovakia and Ruthenia, the Greek Catholic Church had at times been associated with Ruthenian nationalism. So sensitive were the Soviets to this question that in 1947 they executed Bishop Theodor Romza of Uzhgorod (Užhorod), the leading Greek Catholic churchman in the newly annexed territories, and dissolved the church. In Slovakia the church's connections to nationalism were mixed, for a very large number of ethnic Slovaks were Greek Catholics. Nonetheless, the policy inaugurated in the Soviet Union was replicated in Czechoslovakia, and the church was abolished.

An underground Greek Catholic Church apparently existed in eastern Slovakia from that time on, and eighteen years later its adherents came out into the open to demand the legal re-establishment of their church. A riotous situation developed in certain districts around Prešov and Košice during the Prague Spring, and the Dubček government found itself obliged to ap-prove the revival of the Greek Catholic Church or else face grow-ing disorder in the region. The church has continued to exist to this day, although its activities are circumscribed by the same political controls operating over other religious organizations.

The forms of antireligious harassment are less violent today than they were in the Stalin era, but they are no less per-vasive. Members of the clergy must have permits to minister, and these can be withdrawn at any time. Priests and ministers are sometimes imprisoned if they distribute religious literature without the express permission of the state. Seminaries are tightly controlled, and many qualified applicants are arbitrarily turned away despite continuous shortages of clergymen. (One-third of all Catholic parishes are without a priest, and four bish-ops are barred from office.) Most clergymen have come to accept the state's control meekly, although seven Protestant ministers and one Roman Catholic priest were among the signers of Charter 77.

A partial easement of church-state tensions became ap-parent in 1977 with the government's agreement to the appoint-ment of a cardinal in Prague. After a three-year hiatus in which Czechoslovakia had no cardinal, the state finally agreed to allow the Vatican to elevate František Tomášek to this rank. The event was particularly significant because of Tomášek's back-ground: he had spent the years 1951–54 in prison, and to this day he has displayed a moderate degree of independence by refusing to join Pacem in Terris.

Cardinal Tomášek notwithstanding, official pressures on the churches continue, and there were reports of new harassments in the autumn of 1979. The pressures are felt by clergy and laity alike: on occasion, churchgoers have lost their jobs because of their faith, and their children can expect difficulties if they seek admission to higher education. It is especially difficult for religious persons to become teachers because the Party wishes to prevent the "contamination" of the young. This concern produces a contradictory policy with respect to the teaching of religion. The state provides for religious instruction within the school system, but students are discouraged from enrolling in the classes. The state thus aims to turn the younger generation away from religion in the hope that religious orientations will pass from the scene along with the older generation.

It appears that the antireligious strategy is having a partial success. The threat of being barred from higher education effectively persuades many young people who might otherwise attend church not to do so. At the same time, secularizing forces in modern society draw many people naturally away from a religious outlook. On Sundays one finds relatively few young people in Czechoslovakia's churches except in the rural areas, where the pull of tradition is still strong and the pressures of Party rule are less severe. There is evidence, on the other hand, that an increasing number of young people are attracted to secret worship services in "catacomb churches"—illegal, private gatherings in small rooms and apartments. The extent of these meetings is not known, though one might surmise that the groups are few in number and small in membership. Still, their existence—like that of the Charter 77 proponents—is a sign that the regime has not eliminated organized dissent groups, and the fact that practicing Catholics and Protestants are active among chartists underscores their mutuality of interest.[7]

SOCIAL STRUCTURE

In the traditional Marxist-Leninist view, a person's position in a capitalist social structure is dictated by whether he or she is a worker or an employer. The value system of capitalist society is determined by greed and power hunger, and a very high value is accorded to status and prestige, which are measured by income and consumption as well as by subjective attitudes of class and rank. The owners and managers monopolize wealth and indulge in conspicuous consumption; so long as they rule, they also dictate the dominant value patterns of their society and ensure that their prestige is upheld by those values.

In a socialist society, the elimination of the worker-employer dichotomy should lead to an equalization of wealth. This in turn should cause the disappearance of the bourgeois obsession with status and prestige, and in the long run society should experience a lessening of social differentiation. Contributing to this process would be the increasing productivity of the industrial sector, making more and more goods available for the workers. Collective agriculture would transform peasants and farmers into a rural proletariat, thereby eliminating the peasantry as a separate class. The old traits of the bourgeoisie—greed, personal acquisitiveness, and individual self-advancement—would eventually be replaced by socialist values such as egalitarianism and an overriding concern for the welfare of the community rather than that of the individual.

Social Stratification

In socialist Czechoslovakia, the leveling of society began with the radical economic policies of the Third Republic and intensified after 1948. The main policies were the nationalization of industry, rural land reform and collectivization, and a series of draconian monetary reforms that wiped out personal savings and financially crippled the middle and upper strata. Wages and salaries became more nearly equalized, and educational opportunities were expanded for many who previously had little or no access to them. The overall result was a significant reduction of socioeconomic stratification in the traditional sense, a general condition that persisted until the late 1960s.

There were, of course, important exceptions to this tendency. Men tended to receive higher incomes than women, even when occupying positions of comparable responsibility. Pensioners' incomes were very low, often barely above the level of a crude subsistence. At the opposite end of the scale, numerous individuals were able to get rich through a variety of legal and illegal means—black marketeering, currency speculation, or in some cases through an inheritance from the legendary uncle who struck it rich in Chicago. High political officials assumed for themselves the right to certain presocialist perquisites of power: high incomes, luxury apartments and villas, gourmet foods, fine wines, French cognac, and chauffeur-driven limousines.

In the 1970s there appeared to be a general trend toward greater income differentiation. This resulted from the government's policy of encouraging individual enrichment as a distraction from the political stringencies of post-Dubček "normalization." Interestingly, a number of cooperative farmers joined the growing ranks of legitimate millionaires by taking advantage of agricultural subsidies and favorable tax laws. At the same time, the plight of the poorest members of society was exacerbated by inflation. Nor has this problem been confined to an insignificant proportion of the populace; the official count of persons receiving various forms of pensions (old age, invalids', widows', orphans') totaled nearly 25 percent of the country's population as of the mid-1970s.[8] Many of these probably have additional means such as family support, but many others do not and are therefore forced to live on their meager pensions. These facts do not negate the continuing reality that, compared to most Western countries, Czechoslovakia is still characterized in general by a relative equality of incomes and material lifestyles. The discrepancies and anomalies are nonetheless damaging to the regime's self-image and, contrary to theory, they are by no means diminishing as society supposedly approaches the stage of developed socialism.

In any event, the social structure is obviously more complex than a strict interpretation of Marxist-Leninist theory would suggest. Soviet theorists, for example, argue that their society consists today of two classes, the proletariat and the peasantry. Although there is an important distinction within the proletariat between manual laborers and so-called mental workers (administrators, intellectuals, accountants, and so on), Soviet theorists maintain that the differences are politically unimportant and gradually diminishing. This view of social structure predominated in Czechoslovakia during the 1950s, but it came under fire in the 1960s by sociologists and social theorists.

Led by Dr. Pavel Machonin, the sociologists conducted a lengthy and detailed study of Czechoslovak society. Basing their approach on both objective measures and the subjective self-identification of the respondents to their surveys, Machonin and his colleagues discovered a subtle but complex pattern of social differentiation and stratification. On what they termed a horizontal scale, they found that social grouping took place around such factors as occupation, education, geographic locale, ethnicity, and other largely objective denominators, as well as subjective factors such as lifestyles and leisure-time pursuits. Growing out of these factors, and to some extent connected also with income levels, was a measurable *vertical* scale of social stratification and prestige as perceived by the respondents. Thus, for example, high prestige was attached to highly educated persons holding professional positions who lived in urban Bohemia and enjoyed going to the opera; if these persons also happened to have relatively high incomes, that fact tended to lend them increased status, although income itself was not found to be a dominant variable. On the other hand, low status was attached to persons who were relatively uneducated, held unskilled jobs, earned low incomes, and spent all their spare time in pubs. Between these extremes, the sociologists found many variations and constructed a scale of six major social strata ranked in order of their generally perceived status within society. Of course, the multiple variables the sociologists used to measure status led further to an almost infinite number of possible combinations, giving the picture of social stratification a complexity that almost defied measurement.

The work of the Machonin group in many respects paralleled similar research in Poland, Hungary, and Yugoslavia but went farther in its implications. Moreover, Machonin's findings converged with the movement for major political reform and gave that movement added momentum. It provided empirical grounds for Zdeněk Mlynář and others to argue the need for a pluralist structure: if society is really so complex, Mlynář argued, then it is wrong and undemocratic to assume that a monolithically organized state and party can adequately serve the needs of this diverse society. Thus the work of the sociologists underlay one of the most radical issues of the Prague Spring, the democratization of the political sturcture and the broadening of citizen participation.

Largely because of its political implications, the work of Machonin and his colleagues became officially discredited in the post-1968 "normalization." In fact, sociology itself has been treated with great suspicion in the 1970s. The major sociologists of the 1960s lost their positions and joined the ranks of other intellectuals who were banished from the academies. Some sociological writing has been continued in their absence, but these works have been few in number and weak in theory. The resultant gap in sociological knowledge has left the social theorists of the Husák era in confusion about the true nature of Czechoslovak society. The official mainstream has returned to the Soviet position, acknowledging only a broad class of collective farmers and a proletariat subdivided into manual and mental workers. Some scholars remain, however, who insist that the proletariat may contain as many as five strata, and that the intelligentsia—the mental workers—can be broken down into even more numerous substrata.[9] Thus, despite some official opinions to the contrary, Czechoslovak society continues to reveal a complexity that belies the old ideological formulas.

Town and Country

Socialism and the processes of modernization have caused a significant shift in the geographic distribution of the population. Cities have mushroomed as the industrial work force has grown (see Table 5.6); rural areas, transformed by the collective movement and by the mechanization of agriculture, have lost population. The change has been especially noticeable in Slovakia, long a predominantly rural province but now becoming more and more urbanized. This fundamental demographic change, urbanization, has had an important impact on the flavor of life in Czechoslovakia.

Traditionally, the differences between town and countryside were quite substantial. The cities and larger towns were cosmopolitan, cultured, and relatively "modern" in flavor. This

TABLE 5.6
Population Growth of 25 Largest Cities, 1930-1977

City	1930	Population 1960	1977[a]	Percent Increase 1930-77	1960-77
Prague	848,823	1,003,341	1,182,853	39.3	17.8
Brno	271,521	314,379	365,837	34.7	16.4
Bratislava	156,476	242,091	357,574	128.5	47.7
Ostrava	186,545	234,671	319,688	71.4	36.2
Košice	70,117	79,581	191,015	172.4	140.0
Plzeň	130,589	137,763	165,351	26.6	20.0
Olomouc	66,440	70,116	99,013	49.0	41.2
Havířov	b	50,652	93,516		84.6
Hradec Králové	37,519	55,147	90,882	142.2	64.8
Pardubice	31,893	52,655	90,230	182.9	130.9
České Budějovice	60,225	63,949	86,170	43.1	34.7
Liberec	76,181	65,267	83,859	10.1	28.5
Karviná	35,408	46,842	81,864	131.2	74.8
Gottwaldov	27,334	54,189	81,129	196.8	49.7
Ústí Nad Labem	70,319	63,819	77,431	10.1	21.3
Nitra	21,283	34,242	69,340	225.8	102.5
Prešov	21,775	35,121	65,858	202.4	87.5
Kladno	44,238	49,561	63,827	44.3	28.8
Žilina	20,476	32,512	63,647	210.8	95.8
Karlovy Vary	53,913	42,819	61,495	14.1	43.6
Most	30,152	44,490	61,185	102.9	37.5
Banská Bystrica	11,347	22,590	59,330	422.9	162.6
Opava	48,190	42,523	57,937	20.2	36.2
Trnava	23,948	31,732	57,125	138.5	80.0
Martin	8,615	22,440	53,511	521.1	138.5

Source: Statistická Ročenka for 1957, 1961, and 1978. Percent increase was calculated by the author.

[a]Estimate at year's end.

[b]No data available.

was particularly true of Prague, with its large German population, a modestly influential Jewish community, and, from the late nineteenth century on, a flourishing cultural life. Other cities—Plzeň, Brno, Bratislava, Košice—were never the cultural equals of Prague, but they shared with the capital city its ethnic heterogeneity and bustling pace of life. In the villages life was slower-paced, "high" culture was unfamiliar, and attitudes were traditionally oriented. The differences between town and country tended to be less pronounced in Bohemia and stronger in

Slovakia; the difference between Prague and rural Slovakia was that of two societies each foreign to the other.

These differences have not disappeared altogether, but the pattern of accelerated demographic shifting since 1945 has brought the two societies closer together. Many villages have grown into towns while many others have simply died; the total number of villages declined by one-third between 1949 and 1975, owing to abandonment and the merger of rural munici- palities. More importantly, the nature of the village economy has changed as mechanized agriculture has required fewer and fewer laborers. Much as in modern capitalist societies, farmers have become a very small proportion of the population, amount- ing to only 8.5 percent of the total by 1971. Today, the majority of the people who live in villages are employed in nonagricul- tural production, either working in nearby factories or (in very many cases) commuting longer distances to cities and provincial towns for their livelihood.[10]

The physical quality of life is now relatively favorable in the countryside. Average incomes are equal to those in the cities, and in certain respects the standard of living in the vil- lages is higher. Housing, for example, is more readily available than in the cities, where a severe shortage of apartments is an endemic condition of urban life. Rural families own more auto- mobiles and motorcycles per household than do urban dwellers; the same is true of numerous other artifacts of convenience living such as washing machines, deep-freeze units, electric mixers, and sewing machines.

The rising standard of living in the villages is not exclusively caused by the fact that peasants have increasingly traded in their plows and pitchforks for jobs on the assembly line. Im- provements in agricultural productivity, combined with the smaller numbers of collective and cooperative farm workers, have increased the incomes of these workers. In fact, in the 1970s it became well known that a small number of collective farmers had quietly become quite rich over the years, and they now began to display their wealth by purchasing high-cost luxury cars (such as the elite and elegant Czech-made Tatra limousine) and taking vacation trips to America.

Communist officials may not be ecstatic over the existence

of peasant millionaires, but they are generally pleased with the progress toward the elimination of differences between towns and rural areas. And although the regime admits that a similar process has been underway in the capitalist world, the Party accredits its own policies with the success in Czechoslovakia. By having collectivized agriculture and encouraged modern farming methods, those policies have simultaneously improved food production and released labor forces for work in industry. As the occupational structure of the countryside became more mixed, and as town and country dwellers interacted with one another on a daily basis, the villages came to share in the modern orientations and the material standards of the cities.

While rural life has improved greatly, urban life has also continued to hold its own kind of appeal. To those who value the nearness of theaters and music halls, a shortage of living space and the frustrations of traffic congestion are a price worth paying for the amenities of city life. These folks would, in all probability, prefer a quiet café or a sixteenth-century wine cellar to a village pub, and they would not mind sharing their daily walk through the park with numerous other strollers or joggers. They might not object to riding a packed streetcar to work and back, or if they happen to live in Prague near one of the new subway lines, they would likely delight in using this new and convenient form of transportation. Much as they did in the past, today's city dwellers still tend to view villagers as bumpkins—affluent bumpkins, perhaps, but bumpkins nonetheless—and take it for granted that their more highly cultured, if overcrowded, urban environment represents a higher level of civilization than that of their country cousins.

On weekends, however, they are likely to display some ambivalence in this judgment as they leave town for their own holiday cottages. During the time of the First Republic, the Czech bourgeoisie commonly owned private cottages in the country, where they spent many of their leisure hours. In the late 1960s and 1970s, ownership of holiday cottages became very widespread, and the goal of owning one was suddenly a general concern of workers. Many areas of the countryside, especially in scenic regions such as the Šumava mountains or along the upper Vltava River, are now dotted with private cottages. Most of them were built by the owners out of scarce building materials in some cases bought on the black market or pilfered from construction industries. Collectively, they are a monument to the desire for a little piece of privacy away from the hurly-burly of crowded residential districts, the pressures of work, and the red tape of an ever-present bureaucracy.

SUMMARY

Like its geography, the society of modern-day Czechoslovakia is something of a mosaic. Patterns of social differentiation are less glaring than they were before the socialist revolution, but they are no less complex for all their subtlety. Ethnic and national differences no longer provoke the open conflict that characterized earlier periods, but they persist as factors that condition citizens' self-perceptions and inhibit the complete social integration of Czechs, Slovaks, Hungarians, and other groups. Social stratification has taken on a subtle form distinct from the social order of the First Republic, and there is evidence that, as Czechoslovakia's society continues to develop, new patterns of social grouping are evolving. The convergence of rural and urban lifestyles tends to counter the effects of social differentiation in one important aspect, although in another sense it creates new social types, such as the peasant-worker and the rich collective farmer.

Religious grouping also contributes to the mosaic of Czechoslovak society, although it is apparent that religious differences are not a very salient factor in the make-up of today's social order. Catholics and Protestants have found common cause in their struggle to preserve their right to worship, and nonbelievers who feel oppressed by the Communist regime share with believers a condition that is in some respects mutual. Yet the special stringencies that the religious suffer—job discrimination, lessened educational opportunities, and so on—serve to place them in their own specific social category and give them a sense of community that differentiates them from others.

NOTES

1. Some of the material discussed in this chapter is drawn from my earlier work, *The Cultural Limits of Revolutionary Politics: Change and Continuity in Socialist Czechoslovakia* (Boulder, Colo.: East European Quarterly, 1979).

2. The term *nation* as used here refers to a community of people who share a common sense of tradition and a desire to control their own political destiny—irrespective of whether or not the nation is in fact self-governing.

3. George Klein, "Ethnicity in the Communist Party Politics of Czechoslovakia," paper presented at the 1979 annual meeting of the American Political Science Association, p. 13. Klein points out that throughout the 1970s Slovaks occupied eight of sixteen ministerial positions and four of eight deputy prime ministerships.

4. *Europa Year Book 1979*, vol. 1 (London: Europa Publications, 1979), p. 522.

5. The Slovak survey was taken in 1968, a time when many people perceived a relaxation of official pressures on the churches. The North Moravian survey was taken in 1962–63, and it is possible that some of the respondents were reluctant to reveal religious sentiments for fear that the information might be used against them. The surveys are discussed in, among other sources, Vladimir V. Kusin, *Political Grouping in the Czechoslovak Reform Movement* (London: Macmillan & Co., and New York: Columbia University Press, 1972), pp. 207–208.

6. This division oversimplifies a situation that also included Catholic "Czechoslovaks" and a small number of Protestant Slovak nationalists. However, the Catholic-nationalist, Protestant-"Czechoslovak" dichotomy corresponded to the image held by many people, especially Slovaks.

7. For two brief but illuminating discussions of religion in contemporary Czechoslovakia, see Janice A. Broun, "Czechoslovakia: A Glimmer of Hope," *America*, vol. 139, no. 7 (September 16, 1978), pp. 150–152, and Kamil Winter, "Christianity in Communist Czechoslovakia," *The Christian Century*, vol. 94, no. 32 (October 12, 1977), pp. 919–920.

8. According to the government-published *Statistical Yearbook* (*Statistická Ročenka*) for 1976, the number of people on pensions was 3,651,000. For a discussion of relative poverty and wealth, see Otto Ulč, "Some Aspects of Czechoslovak Society Since 1968," *Social Forces*, vol. 57, no. 2 (December 1978), pp. 419–435.

9. Ulč, "Aspects of Czechoslovak Society," p. 425.

10. Ibid. Ulč derived this information from several studies made by Czech and Slovak sociologists in 1976–77.

6

Culture and Education

Like its history, Czechoslovakia's cultural traditions reach back many years through numerous high and low points. Art and literature, as well as science and education, have gone through some difficult periods, yielding a heritage that is in many respects discontinuous. Yet one need not speak in condescending terms of Czechoslovak culture. If it is true that neither the Czechs nor the Slovaks have given the world a major tradition comparable to that of England, France, or Germany, it is also true that Czechoslovakia has left its mark noticeably on the cultural universe. Among the many well-known names one could cite as evidence are Hus (theology), Kepler and Brahé (astronomy), Čapek and Kundera (literature), Neruda (poetry), Dvořák (music), Havel and Kohout (drama), Forman and Kadár (film). In addition, one should recall the contributions of numerous Prague citizens whose works are more closely associated with German culture than with Czech, for example Kafka (literature) and Rilke (poetry), both of whom wrote in the German language.

This chapter will begin with a survey of Czech and Slovak traditions in the arts, followed by a discussion of the arts in the Communist period. Finally, we shall take a brief look at the institutions of today's Czechoslovakia through which culture is supported and propagated—the cultural-administrative superstructure, the mass media, and the educational system.

TWO TRADITIONS: FOLK ART AND FINE ART

Running through the historical development of both Czech and Slovak culture is a dual tradition. When one thinks of "art," one usually thinks first of the fine arts—painting, sculpture, architecture, classical music, literature, and so on. Of these there is a firm tradition in Czechoslovakia. At the same time, there exists a rich tradition of folk culture, the culture of the peasantry and commoners that evolved naturally as everyday people strove to embellish their humble lives with artifacts of beauty. In the nineteenth and twentieth centuries, writers and musicians consciously created a kind of dialogue between folk culture and the fine arts as they reached into the folk traditions for themes that inspired their art. Let us look first at the folk tradition and then turn to the fine arts.

Folk Culture

Most Czechs and Slovaks would probably consider their folk art, music, and legends a precious national heritage. The Czech and Slovak cultures were preserved through the long years of outside rule only by the common people, who kept alive their ethnic and local cultures by passing on from generation to generation folk tales, melodies, styles of various handicrafts, peasant architecture, dances, and painting. Because literacy among the peasantry was rare, the stories and music were not written down until the nineteenth century. Dance steps, embroidery and sewing patterns, and architectural plans were all transmitted orally and by demonstration or emulation. Regions and often villages developed their own characteristic styles according to the tastes of their inhabitants and the nature of materials available locally.

It is impossible to pinpoint the moment at which folk art "began"; surely it began in different localities at different times. Perhaps it is inaccurate, or at least irrelevant, to speak of its "beginnings," for folk art probably evolved originally from the more or less accidental discovery that clothing, tools, and other functional objects could be made interesting by varying something in their design. Certainly, much of the folk art tradition consists of everyday objects such as bowls, drinking mugs, pitchforks, saddles, furniture, and articles of clothing that came to be embellished with designs that were painted, carved, or sewn on them. Houses and other buildings also displayed a flair for functional beauty. Churches were built not only to serve as gathering places but also to glorify God through the rustic adornments provided by local talents. Outdoor shrines, grave markers, and icons added to the lore of religious art.

As far as luxuries were concerned, the peasant had few if any; certainly there were no gold or silver objets d'art such as were prized by the nobility. The luxuries of the peasants consisted of a few simple objects that transcended their everyday necessities and received special artistic attention: fine lace, intricately embroidered dresses and suits for ceremonial occasions, woven tapestries and pillow cases for use only in the "clean room" reserved for guests. Usually these were the work of the womenfolk, oftentimes of the grandmother who had time on her hands because she could no longer do many of the heavy chores that occupied the rest of the family from dawn to dusk.

Folktales, as elsewhere in the world, formed part of an oral tradition that mixed together elements of legend, mythology, fact, religion, and superstition, as well as didactic lessons and explanations of natural and supernatural phenomena. Perhaps the most famous folktales are those told about the legendary Slovak hero Juraj Janošík, a Robin Hood–like character who stole from the rich to help the poor. In real life, Janošík carried on his career of brigandage for only about two years in the early eighteenth century before he was captured and executed. The stories about him, however, proliferated and took on many variations.

Common to most folktales and to folk music as well were themes that derived from the everyday experiences of the peasants. A number of Czech folk songs, for example, sing of young men going off to war to fight for a distant ruler while their lovers are left alone. A well-known Slovak song, "Tancuj, tancuj" (Dance, dance) encourages the singer's partner to dance but cautions him not to disturb the oven on which people must sleep in order to stay warm—because "not everyone has an eiderdown":

Tancuj, tancuj, vykrucaj, vykrucaj,	Dance, dance, whirl, whirl,
len mú piecku nezrucaj, nezrucaj;	Just don't disturb, disturb
dobrá piecka na zimu, na zimu—	my oven;
nemá každý perinu, perinu!	A good oven in the winter,
	in the winter—
	Not everyone has an eiderdown,
	eiderdown!

An interesting Czech folk song tells of the confusion caused by the mixing of ethnic groups. Czechs and Germans had different names for the same town, Domažlice (Taus), leading to the following verse:

Žadnej neví, co jsou Domažlice,	Nobody knows what
žadnej neví, co je to Taus;	Domažlice is,
Taus je to německy, Domažlice	Nobody knows what Taus is;
česky,	Taus—that's German,
žadnej neví, co je to Taus.	Domažlice Czech,
	Nobody knows what Taus is.

Modernization has taken its toll on the folk culture of Czechoslovakia. The simple stories and melodies that were so in tune with traditional peasant life no longer speak to the daily concerns of most Czechs and Slovaks, and the more rapid pace of modern society leaves very few people with the time to keep up the old arts as a hobby. Nevertheless, in recent years the state has encouraged and supported efforts to preserve the artifacts of folk culture lest they be lost forever. Specialized museums exist for the collection and display of folk art; especially noteworthy among them are the Slovak National Museum in the historic town of Martin and the folklore section of the National Museum in Prague. Many musical groups keep alive the country's folk music, and some regularly go on international tours to perform. Handicraft cooperatives have been organized to produce articles of folk costume and other traditional goods, for the government has found that such items sell very well in the tourist shops of Prague and Bratislava.

More important than the manufacture of folk items for sale to tourists is the preservationist ethic. With the state's encouragement, Czechs and Slovaks have become aware that, notwithstanding the glitter of modern manufactured products, there is something of great value in the artful work of their ancestors. Much effort, for example, has gone into the restoration of old peasant houses in some villages, despite the fact that modern homes are more comfortable and might otherwise be more appealing to the villagers. No one is inclined to reject the conveniences of the machine age in favor of a return to wooden clothes paddles and hand-woven everyday clothes, but the citizens of modern-day Czechoslovakia do appreciate the simple beauty of their folk heritage and take pride in the objects handed down by their ancestors.

Literature and the Fine Arts to 1800

Because of the Hungarian domination, the Slovaks did not develop a tradition in literature and the fine arts for many centuries. Czech became the literary language of Slovakia during the Hussite period, and prior to the times of the national awakening the most important Slovak literary work was a Latin chant book written by J. Tranovský in 1676. A few splendid works of architecture were created in the Gothic period, most notably the magnificent churches in Levoča and Bardejov. One of the finest carved-wood altars in all of Europe is to be found in the church of Levoča, the work of the late–fifteenth-century master Pavol (Paul).

In Bohemia, an already firm tradition in the arts had evolved by the Gothic period and continued to develop until 1620. The earliest known literature dates from the end of the tenth century and consists of Latin chronicles written by monks. The first major work in the Czech language were the chronicles of Dalimil (c. 1310). These were followed in the mid-fourteenth century by the philosophical writings of the moralist Tomáš of Štítný, and later by the allegories of Smil Flaška (1394). In the fifteenth century, Jan Hus and Petr Chelčický added to the national literature with their theological writings. The stabilization of Bohemia following the Hussite Wars encouraged the rise of a "golden age" in Czech literature, and the sixteenth century saw a flourishing of Czech prose. Daniel Adam of Veleslavín and Jiří Melantrich are the most significant names associated with this period, and the famous Kralice Bible, the work of several sixteenth-century scholars, became the Czech counterpart of Luther's German Bible and the (later) King James Version in English. The final major figure of Czech letters during this time was Comenius (Komenský), most of whose important writings were published during his exile following the defeat of Bohemia in 1620.

In art and architecture, an even longer tradition can be traced. Aside from scattered art works dating from the Stone Age up to the Middle Ages, the Romanesque period yielded the earliest major works. Still intact to this day are numerous Romanesque structures, notably the church of St. George and other parts of the Prague Castle, as well as rotunda chapels in Prague's Vyšehrad, in Znojmo, and elsewhere. The Gothic period saw a great deal of construction, sculpture, and painting, especially in the fourteenth century. Here again, Prague led the way: outstanding examples of Gothic architecture are the Old Town Hall, the Týn Church in Old Town, the Charles Bridge, and of course the Cathedral of St. Vitus, the last-mentioned being the work of Matthias of Arras and Peter Parler. Outside Prague, many towns and cities took on their shape during the Gothic era and can be seen today as interesting examples of late-medieval "urban planning." Here and there, striking individual pieces of Gothic architecture still remain, for example the unusual church of St. Barbara in Kutná Hora and Charles IV's lavish country castle, Karlštejn. Other forms of art produced during this era were sculptured and painted altarpieces, frescoes, manuscript illuminations, and paintings, as well as the works of a few talented goldsmiths and silversmiths.

The influence of French and especially Italian artists was strong throughout the Gothic era and continued into the Renaissance period. Unlike in Italy, however, the Renaissance style failed to dominate Bohemian art of the sixteenth century but instead mixed with the strong and persistent Gothic patterns. Nevertheless the influence of the Renaissance can be seen in such examples as the Vladislav Hall of the Prague Castle (1493), the Belvedere summer palace (mid-sixteenth century), and many structures in provincial towns, for example the fine town hall of Tábor. That great patron of the arts, Rudolf II, brought to Prague many foreign works of art during this time, some of which are now housed in the National Gallery.

The baroque period is, of course, associated with the "darkness" of Czech culture. One noteworthy Czech painter, Karel Škréta, contributed to the output of the late seventeenth century, but otherwise the art of the baroque was produced by foreigners. This is not to say that the baroque period was a time of artistic decay. On the contrary, the late baroque in particular was a time of monumental construction, sculpture, and painting in Bohemia. Prague became a favorite residence of many wealthy aristocrats who built large palaces with exquisite formal gardens. The city's charming Little Quarter (Malá strana) arose at this time, studded with outstanding and often very original baroque buildings. Magnificent and ostentatious churches, such as St. Nicholas in the Little Quarter, arose and were adorned by the work of Matyáš Braun, Petr Brandl, and others. The architects who contributed to Prague's baroque included Giovanni Santini, K. I. Dientzenhofer, and Johann Fischer von Erlach.

Music also has a lengthy tradition, beginning with a tenth-century Czech hymn, "Hospodine, pomiluj ny" (God Have Mercy Upon Us). Songs and hymns of the Hussites, many of them still sung in churches today, added to the religious music of the Bohemian Reformation, and more religious music was composed by both Protestants and Catholics in the sixteenth century. Three notable sixteenth-century composers of organ music were Jiří and Václav Rychnovský and Jan Trojan Turnovský. Several noble families established their own orchestras, and the patron Rudolf II assembled a fine court orchestra and choir. This promising musical development was interrupted by the Bohemian defeat, although a handful of Czech musicians made significant contributions to the music of the baroque period. The names František V. E. Brixi, Bohuslav Černohorský, and Václav J. Tomášek are among the Czech composers of the seventeenth and eighteenth centuries, and the Czech émigré Jan Václav Stamic (1717–57) became renowned as the director of the fine court orchestra of Mannheim.

The Arts and the National Awakenings

As we have seen in Chapter 1, the reemergence of Czech and Slovak culture from the end of the eighteenth century on had a great political significance. Aside from this, the artistic outpouring of the period deserves to be noted in its own right.

Patriotic themes can be found in the literature throughout the nineteenth century. These sometimes combined with folk motifs to create works that inspired nationalistic feelings. Beginning with Kollár's *Slávy Dcera* (Daughter of Sláva), a lengthy cycle of sonnets presenting an allegorical vision of Pan-Slavic brotherhood, many literary works emerged that expressed strong political sentiments, for example *Songs of a Slave* (1895) by the Czech poet Svatopluk Čech and *From Beneath the Yoke* (1884) by the Slovak poet Svetozar Hurban-Vajanský. Josef Kajetán Tyl wrote plays that frequently expressed Czech nationalism. Czech folk themes are strong in the poetry of Adolf Heyduk and Eliška Krásnohorská, and in the prose of Karolina Světlá and Božena Němcová, whose novel *Grandmother* (1855) is a literary classic. The influence of Slovak folklore is obvious in the poetry of Ján Botto, Janko Král', and Andrej Sládkovič. Also, for the first time, written collections of folktales and songs appeared in the mid-nineteenth century through the efforts of Karel J. Erben and F. L. Čelakovský, both of whom worked with the folklore of several Slavic cultures.

From among the galaxy of prominent writers who emerged during the awakenings and thereafter, mention must be made of three poets, Karel Hynek Mácha, Jan Neruda, and Pavel Országh-Hviezdoslav, as well as a pivotal figure in the development of literary connections between the Czechs and the rest of Europe, Jaroslav Vrchlický. Mácha was a Czech romantic whose poetry was influenced by Byron and Mickiewicz. Neruda was a gifted writer of not only poetry but prose as well; he has been called "in verse a Czech Heine, and in prose a Czech Dickens."[1] Hviezdoslav, a Slovak who became an ardent advocate of Czech-Slovak political unity toward the turn of the twentieth century, published a wide range of works that included lyric verse, narrative poems, drama, and translations of Shakespeare and numerous other foreign-language literary masterpieces. Vrchlický was a poet who introduced a wide array of metrical forms into Czech literature and also translated many foreign poets' works into Czech.

The nineteenth century saw a flowering throughout all

fields of the arts. Czech music, as we have seen, had not been as completely extinguished during the preceding "darkness" as the other arts, and it achieved unprecedented heights with the emergence of Bedřich Smetana (1824–84), Antonín Dvořák (1841–1904), and Zdeněk Fibich (1850–1900). Of these the greatest international renown was achieved by Dvořák, though it is probably true that Smetana is the favorite composer of Czechs. All three were avid devotees of folk music and incorporated many folk melodies and rhythms into their compositions. Smetana's music is pervaded by the composer's love for his country and nation; his most important operas drew upon Czech legends and popular traditions, and his great symphonic cycle, *Má vlást'* (My Country), written in the 1870s after Smetana had become deaf, is a rich and soulful musical creation that has never ceased to bring tears to the eyes of Czech audiences. Dvořák, Smetana's junior by seventeen years, became a major figure on the world musical scene during his own lifetime, spending three years in America where he wrote, among other pieces, his famous ninth symphony titled *From the New World*. Like Smetana, he was greatly inspired by folk melodies and often worked in the exotic rhythmic idioms of national dances, as in his well-known *Slavonic Dances* (1886). Fibich, the least well-known of the three major nineteenth-century composers, is primarily known for his operatic melodramas, but he also composed many works of grand opera as well as symphonic and instrumental pieces.

Finally, the national awakening in the Czech lands stimulated a new interest in painting. The earliest major figure was Josef Mánes (1820–71), a fine classical painter. The generation that followed him sprouted a number of talented artists who were influenced by Western styles including realism and impressionism. The latter style was best reflected in the paintings of Antonín Slavíček. Perhaps the most original Czech painter in the second half of the nineteenth century was Mikuláš Aleš (1852–1913).

The Modern Period

The flowering of the nineteenth century continued into the twentieth and led to what might be called a second "golden

age" of Czech culture, up to the Second World War. During this
time, Czech art developed along lines common throughout
Europe, while a number of artists at the same time explored
their own variations on the new styles of the modern era.

By the end of the nineteenth century, impressionism had
largely given way to art nouveau/Jugendstil, although one of
the most important twentieth-century Czech painters, Max
Švabinský (d. 1961), continued to show the influence of impressionism in his work. Expressionism, cubism, and surrealism
in their times permeated the development of the visual arts.
Groups of artists collected primarily in three cities—Prague and
Brno in the Czech lands and Bratislava in Slovakia. Groups
formed, beginning with The Eight, a Prague-based cubist school
that presented its first exhibition in 1908. As outside influences
mingled with national traditions in varying ways, more groups
came into being—the Artists' Group (1911), the Hardheads
(1919), and later the Mánes group, the Arts Center, and a small
but influential surrealist group in the 1930s.

In literature, a similar progression of styles took place,
from realism to lyricism and impressionism, expressionism, and
surrealism.[2] In independent Czechoslovakia, voices from the
political Left were heard within literary circles; these included
the important Czech poet Vítězslav Nezval and a circle of
Slovak poets, including Laco Novomeský and others who would
remain active in the Communist era, grouped around the periodi-
cal *Dav* (The Masses) from 1925 on. Special mention might be
made of several pre–World War I writers such as the Czech poet
Otakar Březina, the poet-novelist Fráňa Šrámek, Slovak poet
Janko Jesenský, and the émigré Slovak writer of novels and
short stories Martin Kukučin, whose break with the longstand-
ing Slovak tradition of romanticism had an important influence
on subsequent Slovak writers. A great many writers from the
interwar period could be mentioned, including Czechs Vladislav
Vančura and Marie Majerová and the Slovak Martin Rázus.

Three names stand out from the crowd: Franz Kafka,
Jaroslav Hašek, and Karel Čapek. Of Kafka (1883–1924), little
need be said here. His stature as a world literary figure is surpassed by few Europeans of the twentieth century. A Jew who
wrote in German, Kafka did not belong to a "Czech" tradi-

tion, yet his influence on subsequent generations of Czech writers has been profound. Kafka's contemporary Jaroslav Hašek (1883–1923) published relatively few works, but he left the world a major novel of political and social satire, *The Adventures of the Good Soldier Švejk and His Fortunes in the World War*. *The Good Soldier Švejk* has been translated into many languages and can be read as an antiwar novel, as a protest against bureaucracy or social convention, or (arguably) as a piece of sociological fiction that yields much insight into the Czech national character.[3]

It is difficult to summarize the literary contribution of Čapek (1890–1938), for it spans several forms: short stories, novels, drama, travel sketches, and miscellaneous works such as his *Conversations with T. G. Masaryk*. His writings included children's stories, detective stories, and important works of science fiction such as *War with the Newts*. Čapek's style was eclectic, at times clearly reflecting realism and at times exploring the fantastic. He remains to this day the best-loved national author of the Czechs.

Čapek's plays were the culmination of a theatrical tradition that had developed since the mid-nineteenth century. In addition to Čapek, important dramatists of the first half of this century included František Langer and Jiří Mahen. Theatrical life centered around the National Theaters of Prague and Bratislava, but smaller groups sprang up and contributed to a pattern of experimental theater that would be resumed and intensified in the 1960s. A notable example during the interwar period was the so-called Liberated Theater founded by Jan Werich, Jiří Voskovec, and Jaroslav Ježek.

Werich and Voskovec also became active in the newest art, filmmaking, which had its origins in Czechoslovakia in 1919. The Czech cinema experienced mixed beginnings; quite a number of films were produced during the silent era, but despite the interest in foreign avant-garde trends, it was not until the advent of the "talkies" that Czech filmmaking blossomed as an art form of high quality. At this point, several important directors emerged—Martin Frič, Otakar Vávra, and Gustav Machatý, the last-mentioned known for his erotic movies *Erotikon* (1929) and *Ecstasy* (1932) and for the introduction of the glamorous actress Hedy Lamarr to the world cinema scene. There is a distinct line of continuity from this early period of filmmaking to that of the vaunted "Czech miracle" in the 1960s, for several directorial careers spanned both eras—notably those of Vávra and Elmar Klos.

In music, a second generation of national composers came into the spotlight, carrying forward the older tradition and exploring new directions. Two of Dvořák's students, Vítězslav Novák and Josef Suk, were especially noteworthy, as was Otakar Ostrčil, a student of Fibich. Another important name is that of Josef Bohuslav Foerster, who spent the first half of his career abroad, returning to his newly-independent country in 1918. These musical artists, in turn, taught a third generation of musicians and composers that included Otakar Jeremiáš and Alois Hába (students of Novák), Bohuslav Martinů (a student of Suk), and Jaroslav Kvapil (a student of Janáček).

The musical giant of this era was Leoš Janáček (1854–1928). Janáček's activities began in the neoromantic style of Dvořák and Fibich, progressed to a folkloristic trend around the turn of the century, and burst forth into an original and thoroughly modern style that made him an important figure in the avant-garde musical scene. Born in northern Moravia, Janáček studied in Prague, Leipzig, and Vienna before settling in Brno, a provincial city which he made into a significant musical center. His works included operas, symphonic numbers, and choral works, many of them showing the strong influence of his country's folk traditions. Janáček was a key figure in Czech music whose works bridged the nineteenth and twentieth centuries, both in time and in style.

Industrial Arts

Before passing on to the Communist period, a brief word must be said about the industrial arts. Particularly in Bohemia, there exists a long tradition, dating from the eighteenth century, in porcelain and glassworks. The manufacture of art porcelain began in northern Bohemia in 1792, and ever since that time Bohemian china has been highly prized. Bohemian crystal adorned the palaces of the Habsburgs and many other European monarchs, and today the art glass industry produces high-quality products in both cut and blown glass that find their way into exclusive shops throughout the world.

THE ARTS UNDER COMMUNIST RULE

The artistic development that grew out of the free cultural atmosphere of the First Republic was disrupted by the Second World War and stifled by the stringencies of Communist rule. Marxist-Leninists have always valued the arts, but at the same time they have generally sought to emphasize the political utility of artistic endeavors rather than to accept "art for art's sake." Therefore, Communists have tended since the time of Marx to differentiate between "progressive" and "reactionary" art. The former is, of course, preferred because it lends itself to a critical interpretation of prerevolutionary society and a favorable interpretation of socialism. Thus, by definition, "progressive" art is that which promotes a revolutionary and socialist consciousness. In power, the Communists have sought to control the arts in order to ensure the dominance of "progressive" cultural traditions and the demise of "reactionary" and "bourgeois" art.

The Freeze

Efforts to remold Czechoslovakia's artistic patterns reached their apex during the early 1950s, when Soviet-inspired cultural policies dictated that socialist realism be the only acceptable style. Socialist realism, officially defined as the "truthful, historically concrete representation of reality in its revolutionary development," had been the normative mode in the USSR since the First Congress of the Soviet Writer's Union in 1934. In practice, and under the careful guidance of Stalin's cultural dictator, A. A. Zhdanov, socialist realism meant a rigid style that excluded anything but straightforward and simple artistic idioms while restricting the artist to themes of a blunt political nature. Writers and artists were to depict the negative side of capitalism in vivid tones, showing the exploitation of workers, and the positive side of socialism—workers and peasants happily engaged in their labor, stimulated by the collective ethic and optimistically looking forward to communism.

In Czechoslovakia, the first steps toward a stringent cultural policy were taken in 1945, when the Communist Václav Kopecký became minister of culture and sought to redirect the influx of foreign literature to include more Soviet works and fewer from the West. It was some time after the Communist coup that Stalinist policies were applied in their extreme form. When this took place, it meant a radical reorientation of literary and artistic trends, the official encouragement of Russian and Soviet books, and the exclusion of all Western influences except those that fit the regime's official definition of "progressive" forms. For example, Dickens, Balzac, and Dreiser were acceptable because they showed the seamier side of Western society, but most other writers were not; certain classics like the works of Homer, Dante, and Shakespeare were permissible so long as it was understood that they were precursors of socialist realism. Most Western films were excluded, modernist painting and sculpture—especially abstract forms—were strongly condemned, and certain types of modern music were considered decadent, especially jazz and, later, rock and roll. As for Czechoslovakia's own literary past, the regime now sat as judge over the merits of the national traditions; Vančura and Nezval were fine because of their progressive tendencies, but Čapek was discredited and Kafka strictly taboo.

Thus the cultural freeze that had settled over the Soviet Union was spread to Czechoslovakia. Fortunately for Czechoslovak art, the freeze was relatively short-lived, but the official presumption that political utility defines the standards of acceptability in artistic expression continued to impose upon the world of the artist even in the course of the post-Stalin "thaw."

The Thaw

Significantly, the postwar generation of Czech and Slovak intellectuals included many who were committed Communists and who felt dedicated to the task of instilling a revolutionary consciousness in the minds of the workers. The restrictiveness of Stalinist cultural norms was for them a disillusionment, but it did not turn them away from their socialist idealism. Rather, as soon as the political atmosphere showed signs of change, some of the young intellectuals cautiously began to challenge the official norms. Because the political system itself did not change in any fundamental way until 1968, the intellectuals had an uphill fight on their hands. Nevertheless, by 1956 they established their right to venture outside the restrictive boundaries of socialist realism, and in the subsequent decade a gradual process of literary and artistic ferment unfolded. Perhaps it would be an exaggeration to refer to this as a third "golden age," but in many cultural fields the results were exciting and promising. The mid- and late-1960s saw the culmination of these events.

The generation of writers who became prominent during this time was an exceptional group indeed. It included both Czechs and Slovaks, who found common cause in their struggle to create a new literature that was at once artistically sophisticated and politically progressive. Among the Slovaks who were important in this movement were Laco Novomeský, by this time an old man, and Ladislav Mňačko. The latter was a fiery novelist who on several occasions openly challenged the regime's right to impose restrictions on literary freedom. His novel *The Taste of Power* (1966) was a stunning realist critique of Communist rule, focusing on the abuse of power in high places. His strong social criticism was echoed in the works of Czech authors such as Ludvík Vaculík (*The Axe*, 1967) and Jiří Mucha, who among other writings contributed a remarkable collection of reminiscences from Stalin-era labor camps, *Living and Partly Living*. Humor was well represented in the writings of Bohumil Hrabal (*Closely Watched Trains, The Pearls in the Abyss,* and *Dancing Lessons for the Older and More Advanced*), as well as those of Josef Škvorecký (*The Cowards*). Eduard Goldstücker, a German Jew born in Slovakia, became active in Prague literary circles following his release from a political prison in the late 1950s and came to lead a hard-fought effort to revive the work of Kafka. Goldstücker's efforts were well received by many of the newer writers who admired Kafka's use of the absurd and employed it in their own writings; among them were the novelist Ivan Klíma and the playwright Václav Havel. Also rehabilitated in the late 1950s were the works of Karel Čapek, which served as the subject of a book-length essay by Klíma in 1962.

The most gifted writer of this generation is Milan Kundera (b. 1929). Kundera's novel *The Joke* (1967) is one of the richest European novels of the twentieth century. It is a tragicomic epic that not only serves as an indictment of Stalinism but also blends in touches of philosophy and religion, a theory of folk music, and above all an introspective look at both the good and the base side of the human personality.

In the world of the theater, the 1960s witnessed the rise of two brilliant major playwrights, Václav Havel and Pavel Kohout. Havel's plays, including *The Garden Party* and *The Memorandum*, have been widely translated and performed internationally, as has Kohout's play *Poor Murderer*. Other significant contributors to dramatic literature were Kundera, Klíma, and the Slovak Peter Karvaš. Prague in particular became an active center of experimental theater during this time, with numerous "little theaters" and cabarets serving to propagate the art. Also important were the contributions of the Prague Mime School and Ladislav Fialka's Theater on the Balustrade, as well as the famed puppet theater of Jiří Trnka.

The "miracle" of the Czechoslovak cinema hit the Western world with a bang in the 1960s. Almost overnight, it seemed as though a marvel of cinematic excellence had sprung from out of nowhere. Czech films ran off with many prestigious awards at the major European film festivals and twice in succession captured Academy Awards in the United States for best foreign film (*The Shop on Main Street* in 1966, *Closely Watched Trains* in 1967). Of course, in reality the films did not come from nowhere; they came from a tradition with deep roots and, in the increasingly freer atmosphere of Czechoslovakia in the sixties, the films reflected the highest aspirations of two filmmaking generations. A remarkably lengthy list of talented directors from this time would have to include, first and foremost, Miloš Forman (*Loves of a Blonde, Firemen's Ball*), who went on to achieve fame in the United States after 1969 for directing *One Flew over the Cuckoo's Nest, Hair,* and other films. In Czechoslovakia, Forman was only one of numerous outstanding directors including Jan Kadár and Elmar Klos (*The Shop on Main Street*), Jiří Menzel (*Closely Watched Trains, Capricious Sum-*

mer), Jan Němec (*Diamonds of the Night, The Party and the Guests*), Vojtěch Jasný (*When the Cat Comes, All My Countrymen*), Ivan Passer (*Intimate Lighting*), Zbyněk Brynych (*And the Fifth Horseman Is Fear*), František Vláčil (*Markéta Lazarová*), Pavel Juráček (*The Case for a Beginning Hangman*), Evald Schorm (*Courage for Every Day*), and one of the world's foremost women directors, Věra Chytilová (*Daisies*). Two important Slovak directors were Štefan Uher and the young, highly original Juraj Jakubisko. Talented screenwriters included many of the aforementioned directors plus Ester Krumbachová, Antonín Máša, and Jan Procházka. A distinguished film critic of this decade was Antonín J. Liehm.

The films evidenced a variety of styles, from the stark realism of Schorm to the stylized absurdism of Chytilová and the abstract metaphor of Němec and Krumbachová's *The Party and the Guests*. Almost no subject was taboo, from love to politics, and indeed a number of films courageously explored highly sensitive political questions. For example, Schorm and Máša's *Courage for Every Day* traces the ideological disillusionment of an exemplary socialist worker amid cynical leader-types and apathetic citizens. Jaromil Jireš directed the movie version of Kundera's *The Joke*, bringing that bold attack on Stalinism onto the screen, while Němec and Krumbachová, in *The Party and the Guests*, examined the psychology of decent citizens who conform to the most absurd and ultimately inhumane dictates of a controlling power.

Contemporary art and music have also had their lively moments, though in neither case have any individual giants emerged comparable to Dvořák or Janáček. Still, a number of composers have carried on the musical tradition of the national masters; among them have been Václav Dobiáš, Jan Seidel, and Klement Slavický. Czechoslovakia has quite a number of symphony orchestras, permanent opera companies, choral groups, and smaller ensembles; numerous conductors have achieved an international reputation, most notably Rafael Kubelík, Karel Ančerl, and Václav Neumann. Music schools in Prague, Brno, and Bratislava have trained many professional musicians, some of whom have achieved fame as soloists throughout the world.

Prague in the 1960s was an exciting city, full of young

artists displaying their paintings and drawings in cafés and al-fresco galleries. Students and intellectuals gathered in the cafés to hear new poets read their latest creations and in the "little theaters" to see officially frowned-upon experimental or satiri-cal drama. Jazz had made a return to respectability in the late 1950s and could be heard in the fashionable hangouts of the younger generation.

The literati inevitably were drawn into politics. They worked from within their professional associations to encourage a freer cultural climate, but many of them ineluctably came into conflict with the political authorities and their appointed guardians of culture. Mňačko's *Taste of Power* was denied pub-lication for two years after it was written. Schorm, Chytilová, and Němec evoked the ire of the authorities with their films. Havel's plays were performed, but they were not officially loved. *Literární noviny* (Literary News), the main newspaper of the Czechoslovak Writers' Union, frequently clashed with the authorities until it was taken over by the Ministry of Culture and Information following the momentous Fourth Congress of the Czechoslovak Writers' Union in 1967. At that congress, strong denunciations of the government's policies were voiced by Vaculík, Klíma, Liehm, and many others, leading to the expulsion of those three persons from the Communist Party. The crisis in the Writers' Union was one of the crucial political confrontations that contributed to the decline of Antonín Novotný's ruling position in the final months of 1967.

Most of the intellectuals continued to play an active politi-cal role during 1968, although some withdrew, welcoming the chance to do their own work without interference from the politicians. Those who were politically active jumped to the forefront of the reform movement. The height of their activities was reached with the circulation of Vaculík's Two Thousand Words, an uncompromising document that sealed the fate of the radical intellectuals in the years following the Soviet-led occupation.

The 1970s

In the seventies it became sadly apparent that the sixties had been the good old days. The increasingly flexible cultural policies of Novotný had in fact been the result of the regime's weakness under the pressure of its own Communist intellectuals. Seeing in artistic freedom the seeds of anarchy, the Husák regime systematically tightened the screws. Kundera, Vaculík, Havel, Liehm, Forman, Němec, Schorm, Kohout, Klíma, Škvorecký, and nearly all other outstanding personalities of the 1960s became personae non gratae, forbidden to publish or make films in their own country. In the course of the decade following the Soviet occupation many of these artists left Czechoslovakia, either voluntarily or by compulsion. Most of those who did not leave—such as Vaculík, Havel, Kundera (until his departure in 1976), and Kohout (who was refused permission to return home from abroad in 1979)—have been forced to seek outlets for their ongoing works in foreign lands. Vaculík and Havel, as we have seen, have become outspoken supporters of Charter 77; in this capacity they have lived their lives under the constant threat of repression, and at the time of this writing Havel himself was behind bars. Only a few personalities from the sixties have thrived in the seventies. Laco Novomeský, a close friend of Husák and a relative moderate in 1968, escaped official sanction and died in favor. Bohumil Hrabal made an official return to publishing in 1976 with his novel *The Haircut*. However, the quality and the fervor of the 1960s have not returned to Czechoslovakia's cultural life.

The one area of literature that maintains a high level of quality is children's literature. For many years Czechoslovakia has produced excellent children's books, largely because many serious writers—from the time of Čapek and Vančura to the present—have written stories for children. In the 1970s, a number of writers who were otherwise not allowed to publish turned to children's stories (for example, Frantisek Lazecký and Hana Ponická) and thus managed to earn a living while keeping their writing skills in practice. Czech film director Karel Kachyňa also turned his talents toward the youngest generation and received an award at Cannes in 1977 for one of his children's films.

In most other fields, the situation is unfavorable. There have been a few exceptions in the filmmaking business, notably the release of two high-quality films by Jireš, *Valerie and the Week of Wonders* (1969) and *And Give My Love to the Swallows*

(1971). Many other films made during the early Husák years were seized by the censors, and the films made throughout the rest of the seventies were mostly undistinguished. A glimmer of hope, however, accompanied the return to filmmaking of Chytilová (*The Apple Game*) and Menzel (*Those Magnificent Movie Men*) in 1979.

Theatrical life also went generally into eclipse after 1968, although there has been an interesting ferment in the provincial theaters since the late 1970s, especially in Plzeň and Cheb. In addition, four Slovak playwrights have caught the attention of the theater-going public—Oswald Zahradník, Ivan Bukovčan, Jan Kakoš, and Jan Solovič. Beyond these new lights, however, the current stage lacks a lively contemporary flair and must rely on classics to draw appreciative crowds.

In literature, of course, the underground Padlock series offers one way of getting works printed and circulated. This illegal circulation, while not narrow, fails to reach the broadest possible readership that the dissident writers yearn to reach. The underground press is therefore a less-than-satisfying medium but still a precious vehicle for creating the literary dialogue that otherwise could not be carried on.

As in other aspects of policy, the current regime prefers cultural quiescence to an inspired and potentially rambunctious intelligentsia. In the long run, officials hope they can regenerate a socialist art that will reflect a "correct" balance between collective and individual problems. In the recent words of one spokesman, Czechoslovak art and literature still have an "extraordinarily important ideological duty" to perform among the workers.[4] Past experience suggests that this will be extremely difficult in the absence of greater intellectual freedom.

ORGANIZATION OF CULTURE AND EDUCATION

The Czechoslovak Socialist Republic has tended to support the arts and cultural associations rather generously, as the Communists are eager to make the arts available to all citizens. In the closing pages of this book we shall treat some of the most important institutions of culture and education.

Culture and the Arts

The federal Ministry of Culture and Information is the highest governmental body concerned with the propagation of culture. In line with the federal structure of the country, there are separate ministries of culture for the Czech and Slovak Socialist Republics located in Prague and Bratislava, respectively. Those who create the arts—the cultural intellectuals themselves—are organized in professional associations such as the Writers' Union, the Filmmakers' Union, and so on. Most of these now have separate Czech and Slovak branches.

The cultural intellectuals have traditionally occupied a privileged position within society in return for their contribution to socialist culture; their salaries tend to be relatively high, they have priority in the allotment of scarce housing, they enjoy state-funded vacation resorts, and their status is greatly respected by the general public. On the other hand, the privileges can be revoked at the will of the political authorities—as the leading intellectuals of the 1960s discovered in the 1970s. Clearly, the price of a privileged position is loyal service to the state and Party.

The story of the intellectuals and their political challenge during the 1960s is too complex to be adequately told in these few pages, but it points out two things about the role of the arts in socialist societies. In the first place, the arts can be a powerful force when their creators are united behind a common cause—the cause in this case being intellectual freedom, which the artists discovered was inseparable from political freedom more broadly defined. In 1968, a writer for the French newspaper *Le Monde* suggested that if Czechoslovakia's former President Novotný had been asked what writers could do, he would have replied, "Depose me!"[5] Perhaps they did. On the other hand, the arts can be quickly reduced to a derivative position, the servant of the state and little more, if the state insists on closely controlling the artists' media—the publishing houses, theaters, newspapers, film studios, galleries, radio and television networks. Having lost control over these media for one crucial decade, the Party and state are now determined to retain the hold they have reestablished and to "protect" the public against the danger of intellectual dissent.

Mass Communications

Approximately thirty daily newspapers are published in Czechoslovakia, in addition to more than 1,000 other periodicals. All are carefully observed by state authorities in their effort to guarantee the fulfillment of the 1966 press law, which stresses that the information to be published must advance the interest of socialism and enlighten citizens about the Party's policies. Censorship is generally exercised by the editorial staffs of the publications themselves, the heads of which are in all cases chosen for their political reliability. In the 1960s, the policy of self-censorship facilitated the rise of dissident editorial tendencies in a number of important papers (especially *Literární noviny,* which no longer exists), and in 1968 the open political atmosphere encouraged the sudden flowering of a free press. Government censorship was imposed upon the press in 1969 in order to "normalize" the situation, and as editorial staffs were purged of politically unacceptable elements the job of controlling the content of news publications reverted back to the newspapers again. The importation of foreign newspapers is strictly controlled, and in contrast to the more liberal policies of neighboring Hungary, visiting Americans who look for copies of *Time, Newsweek,* or the *International Herald Tribune* will not find them for sale and must instead settle for *Morning Star,* published by the British Communist Party.

Rudé právo (Red Justice) is the main organ of the Communist Party of Czechoslovakia; published in Prague, it has the largest daily circulation in the country, approximately 900,000 copies. The Bratislava daily *Pravda* (circulation 300,000) is the Slovak counterpart to *Rudé právo.* The trade unions publish their own dailies, *Práce* (Labor) in Prague and *Práca* in Bratislava, and the Socialist Union of Youth publishes *Mladá fronta* (Youth Front). The Hungarian-language daily *Új Szó* (New Word), published in Bratislava by the Slovak Communist Party, has a circulation of 85,000. Two of the minor political parties publish their own newspapers—*Lidová demokracie* (People's Democracy) of the People's Party and *Svobodné slovo* (The

Free Word) of the Socialist Party. The country's main news agency is the Prague-based ČTK (*Československá tisková kancelář*, Czechoslovak Press Agency). ČTK is directly controlled by the federal government and acts as its spokesman.

As of the late 1970s there were more than thirty publishing houses in the Czech lands and eighteen in Slovakia. Their activities are mostly run by the government, the political parties, the trade unions, and the professional unions, but religious organizations are also allowed to publish as long as the texts are officially cleared by state authorities. The main organ of religious publication is the Central Churches' Publishing House in Prague. The fact that the Writers' Union had its own publishing house, independently funded through a union tax on royalties, made it possible for the writers of the 1960s to venture into politically sensitive territory, but the purges after 1968 returned the Writers' Union and its publishing house to a position of political conformity.

Five radio networks operate in Czechoslovakia, and radio stations broadcast from Prague, Bratislava, Banská Bystrica, Brno, České Budějovice, Hradec Králové, Košice, Ostrava, Prešov, Plzeň, and Ústí nad Labem. Television studios operate in Prague, Brno, Ostrava, Košice, and Bratislava. Czechs and Slovaks are avid listeners and viewers of radio and television, and almost every household in the entire country has a television receiver and at least one radio. Foreign radio broadcasts are received widely from such Western news and propaganda agencies as the Voice of America, Radio Free Europe, and the British Broadcasting Corporation, as well as from West German and Austrian stations. In southern Moravia and western Slovakia, including Bratislava, Viennese television is easily and clearly picked up. The government has at varying times sought to "jam" Western broadcasts but generally does not do so any more.

Education and Science

The development of education goes back to Comenius and, before his time, to the founding of Prague's Charles University in 1348. The beginning of Czech science also took place centuries ago, and Rudolf II's court astronomers Johannes Kepler and Tycho Brahé were able to base their sixteenth-century work on a scientific tradition that was already 200 years old. In the half-century prior to 1918 much attention was given to the development of education in the Czech lands, and after independence Slovakia profited greatly from the influence of Czech educators.

In the Communist era, education and science have made good progress in many respects, although ideological stringencies have seriously interfered with the development of some fields, especially in the social sciences. The exodus of literally thousands of scholars, scientists, and engineers after 1968, together with the firing of all those who were implicated in the reformist activities of the Dubček months, have badly hampered all fields of inquiry in the years since.

For many children, basic education begins with nursery school from ages three to six. Schooling is compulsory between the ages of six and fifteen, through the ninth grade. Most children continue into secondary school, but there they are "tracked" into either general secondary schools or vocational schools; the majority attend the latter, training them for direct entry into a trade. The general secondary schools prepare their students for higher education and allow them to concentrate their three-year studies in either mathematics and science or languages, humanities, and social science. In addition, there are many secondary schools for adults who have not previously gone beyond elementary school or who desire or need some further schooling. Education at all levels, including higher education, is totally state-supported and free of cost. Needy and especially deserving university students frequently receive stipends to help pay for their living expenses while attending school.

As of 1978, there were thirty-six institutions of higher learning, with a total enrollment of almost 180,000 students. Largest of these is Charles University, with more than 25,000 students. Other universities are the Comenius University in Bratislava, the Palacký University in Olomouc, and the J. E. Purkyně University in Brno. Additional institutions specialize in the fields of economics, engineering and technology, mining and metallurgy, agriculture, forestry, textiles, and veterinary medicine. The main medical school is a branch of Charles University located in Plzeň.

Since its foundation in 1952, the Czechoslovak Academy of Sciences has been the most important research center, together with its more recently established sister institution, the Slovak Academy of Sciences. Both carry on a great deal of research in all fields of science, including the social sciences, and they have an extensive network of libraries, laboratories, and other research facilities. In Slovakia, the Matica slovenská (Slovak Foundation), which was closed down by the Hungarians in 1875, reestablished in 1919, and disbanded by the Communists in 1953, made a comeback in the early 1960s. An institution dear to the hearts of Slovak patriots, the Matica continues to devote its modest efforts to the study of Slovak history and culture.

NOTES

1. Paul Selver, *Czechoslovak Literature: An Outline* (London: Allen & Unwin, 1942), p. 15.

2. A number of modern Czech and Slovak literary works have been translated into English. They include the following:

Karel Čapek, *President Masaryk Tells His Story* [titled in Czech *Conversations with T. G. Masaryk*] (1935; reprint ed., New York: Arno Press, 1971), and *War with the Newts*, trans. M. and R. Weatherall (New York: Berkeley Medallion Books, 1967).

Jaroslav Hašek, *The Adventures of the Good Soldier Švejk and His Fortunes in the World War*, trans. Cecil Parrott (New York: Thomas Y. Crowell Co., 1974).

Václav Havel, *The Garden Party*, trans. Vera Blackwell (London: Cape, 1969) and *The Memorandum*, trans. Vera Blackwell (London: Cape, 1967).

Pavel Kohout, *Poor Murderer*, trans. Herbert Berghof and Laurence Luckinbill (New York: Viking Press, 1975).

Milan Kundera, *The Joke*, trans. David Hamblyn and Oliver Stallybrass (New York: Coward-McCann, 1969).

Ladislav Mňačko, *The Taste of Power*, trans. Paul Stevenson (New York: Praeger Publishers, 1967).

Josef Škvorecký, *The Cowards*, trans. Jeanne Němcová (New York: Grove Press, 1970).

Ludvík Vaculík, *The Axe*, trans. Marian Šling (London: Deutsch, 1973) and *The Guinea Pigs*, trans. Káča Poláčková (New York: Third Press, 1973).

3. See my own rather controversial analysis of this sociological aspect of *Švejk* in David W. Paul, *The Cultural Limits of Revolutionary Politics: Change and Continuity in Socialist Czechoslovakia* (Boulder, Colo.: East European Quarterly, 1979), pp. 256-268.

4. Oldřich Rafaj, in *Tvorba* (Prague), January 3, 1979.

5. Antonín J. Liehm, *The Politics of Culture*, trans. Peter Kussi (New York: Grove Press, 1970), p. 41.

Annotated Bibliography

The following is a list of titles in the English language on Czechoslovakia, selected from a wide-ranging literature. For further references, consult the entries by Sturm, Kusin, and Hejzlar (below).

GENERAL WORKS, MEMOIRS, AND HISTORY TO 1948

Beneš, Eduard. *Memoirs; From Munich to New War and New Victory*. London: Allen & Unwin, 1954.
> Translation of Beneš's prematurely triumphant reflections on the Second World War, written before the Communist takeover.

Bloomfield, Jon. *Passive Revolution: Politics and the Czechoslovak Working Class, 1945–8*. New York: St. Martin's Press, 1979.
> A new book on the Czechoslovak revolution, written from a critical Marxist viewpoint.

Brisch, Hans, and Volgyes, Ivan, eds. *Czechoslovakia: The Heritage of Ages Past*. Boulder, Colo.: East European Quarterly, 1979.
> A sparse and randomly assembled collection of well-written essays on aspects of Czechoslovakia's history from the time of Hus to the present.

Brock, Peter, and Skilling, H. Gordon, eds. *The Czech Renaissance of the Nineteenth Century*. Toronto: University of Toronto Press, 1970.
> A fine collection of essays on the Czech lands under Austrian rule.

Kaminsky, Howard. *A History of the Hussite Revolution*. Berkeley: University of California Press, 1967.
> A scholarly study of Hus and the Hussites.

Korbel, Josef. *The Communist Subversion of Czechoslovakia, 1938–1948*. Princeton, N.J.: Princeton University Press, 1959.
> The Communist coup and its backgrounds.

_____. *Twentieth Century Czechoslovakia: The Meaning of Her History*. New York: Columbia University Press, 1977.
> A thoughtful historical essay by the late diplomat and scholar who left his country after the Communist coup.

Lettrich, Jozef. *History of Modern Slovakia*. New York: Praeger Publishers, 1955.
> One of a very few studies of Slovak history in the English language.

Macek, Josef. *The Hussite Movement in Bohemia*. Prague: Orbis, 1958.
> Monograph written from a scholarly Marxist perspective.

Mamatey, Victor S., and Luža, Radomír, eds. *A History of the Czechoslovak Republic, 1918–1948*. Princeton, N.J.: Princeton University Press, 1973.
> A collection of articles, some of them brilliant, on the political, social, and economic history of this eventful thirty-year period.

Masaryk, Tomáš G. *The Making of a State: Memories and Observations, 1914–1918*. New York: Frederick A. Stokes Co., 1927.
> Detailed memoir of Masaryk's diplomatic efforts leading up to Czechoslovak independence.

Olivová, Věra. *The Doomed Democracy: Czechoslovakia in a Disrupted Europe, 1914–38*. London: Sidgwick and Jackson, and Montreal: McGill-Queen's University Press, 1972.
> Intelligent, Marxist analysis of the independence movement and the First Republic, set within a coherent interpretation of the international environment.

Opočenský, Jan. *The Collapse of the Austro-Hungarian Monarchy and the Rise of the Czechoslovak State*. Prague: Orbis, 1928.
> A detailed account of the formation of Czechoslovakia by a Czech historian.

Rechcígl, Miloslav, Jr., ed. *The Czechoslovak Contribution to World Culture*. The Hague: Mouton, 1964.
> Articles on history, politics, culture, and other subjects.

_____, ed. *Czechoslovakia Past and Present*. The Hague: Mouton, 1968.

Two very thick volumes of articles on a wide variety of topics, written mainly by émigré scholars.

Seton-Watson, Robert W. *History of the Czechs and Slovaks*. Reprint of 1943 ed. Hamden, Conn.: Archon Books, 1965.
General history written by an eminent British scholar, personal friend of Masaryk, and ardent proponent of the "Czechoslovak" theory (discussed in Chapters 1 and 5).

Steiner, Eugen. *The Slovak Dilemma*. Cambridge: Cambridge University Press, 1973.
A short, historical interpretation of Slovakia's special position in Czechoslovakia.

Sturm, Rudolf. *Czechoslovakia. A Bibliographic Guide*. Washington, D.C.: Library of Congress, 1967.
A useful bibliography, though now a bit dated.

Thomson, S. Harrison. *Czechoslovakia in European History*. Princeton, N.J.: Princeton University Press, 1953.
A selective, interpretive history of Czechoslovakia.

Tigrid, Pavel. "The Prague Coup of 1948: The Elegant Takeover." In *The Anatomy of Communist Takeovers*, edited by Thomas T. Hammond, pp. 399–432. New Haven, Conn.: Yale University Press, 1975.
Short but excellent account of the "victorious February" by an émigré scholar-publicist who made use of numerous rare source materials temporarily available during 1968.

Wallace, William V. *Czechoslovakia*. Boulder, Colo.: Westview Press, 1976.
Detailed historical survey by a British author.

Zinner, Paul E. *Communist Strategy and Tactics in Czechoslovakia: 1918–48*. New York: Praeger Publishers, 1963.
A study of the formation, development, and victory of the Communist Party of Czechoslovakia.

THE COMMUNIST PERIOD: POLITICS, SOCIETY, AND THE ECONOMY

Brodský, Jaroslav. *Solution Gamma*. Translated by Káča Poláčková. Toronto: Gamma Print, 1971.
Memoirs of a Czech citizen from his days in a Stalinist prison to the events of 1968.

Brown, Archie, and Wightman, Gordon. "Czechoslovakia: Revival and Retreat." In *Political Culture and Political Change in Communist States*, edited by Archie Brown and Jack Gray. London: Macmillan & Co., and New York: Holmes and Meier, 1977.
    A stimulating article on Czechoslovakia's political culture especially strong on citizens' perceptions of their national history.

Brzezinski, Zbigniew K. *The Soviet Bloc: Unity and Conflict*. Rev. ed. Cambridge, Mass.: Harvard University Press, 1967.
    Detailed and thoroughly documented study of the Soviet bloc, 1945–65, emphasizing political-ideological relations.

Krejčí, Jaroslav. *Social Change and Stratification in Postwar Czechoslovakia*. London: Macmillan & Co., and New York: Columbia University Press, 1972.
    Competent analysis by a distinguished Czech sociologist who was forced into exile after 1968.

Loebl, Eugen. *Stalinism in Prague; The Loebl Story*. New York: Grove Press, 1969.
    Grim, detailed account of life in a political prison, written by a Slovak Communist and one-time prominent economist.

London, Artur. *The Confession*. New York: William Morrow & Co., 1970.
    Another prison story, this one by a Czech who served as foreign minister prior to his arrest. The book was made into a chilling movie by a French film company.

Paul, David W. *The Cultural Limits of Revolutionary Politics: Change and Continuity in Socialist Czechoslovakia*. Boulder, Colo.: East European Quarterly, 1979.
    An eclectic, controversial monograph that looks at continuous patterns in Czechoslovakia's political culture before and after the Communist revolution.

Pelikán, Jiří. *The Czechoslovak Purge Trials, 1950–1954*. Stanford, Calif.: Stanford University Press, 1971.
    An extraordinary book, the translation of a 1968 Party commission's report that followed an extensive and candid investigation of the Stalinist purges.

Richta, Radovan, et al. *Civilization at the Crossroads: Social and Human Implications of the Scientific and Technological Revolution*. White Plains, N.Y.: International Arts and Sciences Press, 1969.

English translation of the 1966 work by Czechoslovak academicians exploring the economic and social implications of modern technology; a highly technical and controversial work that stimulated far-reaching discussions in Czechoslovakia.

Šik, Ota. *Czechoslovakia: The Bureaucratic Economy*. White Plains, N.Y.: International Arts and Sciences Press, 1972.
Translation of a television series broadcast in 1968, in which the noted Czech economist Ota Šik explained and criticized the workings of his country's economic system.

_____. *Plan and Market under Socialism*. White Plains, N.Y.: International Arts and Sciences Press, 1967.
A more technical work than the preceding title, this book spelled out Šik's reformist economic ideas in detail.

Taborsky, Edward A. *Communism in Czechoslovakia 1948–1960*. Princeton, N.J.: Princeton University Press, 1961.
Voluminous study of all aspects of politics and society, written in a cold-war tone but full of factual information painstakingly documented.

Ulč, Otto. *Politics in Czechoslovakia*. San Francisco: W. H. Freeman and Co., 1974.
A very good discussion of the political system from a structural-functional approach contrasting the reforms of 1968 with practices before and after.

_____. "Some Aspects of Czechoslovak Society since 1968." *Social Forces*, vol. 57, no. 2 (December 1978), pp. 419–435.
Brief political-sociological article on the 1970s.

1968

Dean, Robert W. *Nationalism and Political Change in Eastern Europe: The Slovak Question and the Czechoslovak Reform Movement*. Denver, Colo.: Denver University Graduate School of International Affairs. Monograph Series in World Affairs, 1972–73.
Short but perceptive monograph on the Slovaks' role in the events of the reform period.

Golan, Galia. *The Czechoslovak Reform Movement: Communism in Crisis 1962–1968*. Cambridge: Cambridge University Press, 1971.
Detailed study of politics in the years leading up to 1968.

_____. *Reform Rule in Czechoslovakia: The Dubček Era, 1968–1969*.
Cambridge: Cambridge University Press, 1973.
    An intensive study of the reforms, the intervention, and the inter-
regnum to the time of Dubček's removal.

Kusin, Vladimir V. *The Czechoslovak Reform Movement 1968*. Santa
Barbara, Calif.: ABC-Clio, 1973.
    One of several books by an outstanding Czech-émigré political
scientist.

_____. *From Dubček to Charter 77: A Study of "Normalization" in
Czechoslovakia 1968–1978*. New York: St. Martin's Press, 1978.
    Excellent study of the end of the reform government, the policies
of the Husák regime, and the rise of organized dissent in the 1970s.

_____. *The Intellectual Origins of the Prague Spring*. Cambridge: Cam-
bridge University Press, 1971.
    A concise account of intellectual dissent, 1956–68.

_____. *Political Grouping in the Czechoslovak Reform Movement*. Lon-
don: Macmillan & Co., and New York: Columbia University Press, 1972.
    A political sociology of the 1968 events.

Kusin, Vladimir V., and Hejzlar, Zdeněk. *Czechoslovakia 1968–1969:
Annotation, Bibliography, Chronology*. New York: Garland Publishers,
1974.
    A guide to publications on the "Prague Spring" up to 1974.

Littell, Robert, ed. *The Czech Black Book*. New York: Praeger Publishers,
1969.
    Translation of a hastily collected volume of documents, assembled
by Czech historians during the first week following the 1968 occupation, reporting the occupation and public response.

Oxley, Andrew; Pravda, Alex; and Ritchie, Andrew, eds. *Czechoslovakia:
The Party and the People*. London: Allen Lane, 1973.
    Documents of the reform period.

Piekalkiewicz, Jaroslaw A. *Public Opinion Polling in Czechoslovakia,
1968–1969: Results and Analysis of Surveys Conducted During the Dubček
Era*. New York: Praeger Publishers, 1972.
    Interesting sample of the unusual public opinion polls of the reform
period.

Pravda, Alex. *Reform and Change in the Czechoslovak System: January–August 1968*. Beverly Hills, Calif.: Sage Publications, 1975.
Intelligent, theoretically sophisticated monograph on the politics of reform.

Remington, Robin A., ed. *The Winter in Prague: Documents on Czechoslovak Communism in Crisis*. Cambridge, Mass.: M.I.T. Press, 1969.
An early collection of documents from 1968–1969.

Selucký, Radoslav. *Economic Reforms in Eastern Europe: Political Background and Economic Significance*. Translated by Zdeněk Eliáš. New York: Praeger Publishers, 1972.
General survey of East European economic reforms with emphasis on the attempted Czechoslovak reforms. Written by a Czech political economist.

Skilling, H. Gordon. *Czechoslovakia's Interrupted Revolution*. Princeton, N.J.: Princeton University Press, 1976.
To date the definitive study of the reforms and the intervention, this monumental volume is an encyclopedia of carefully documented facts and a disciplined analysis of the 1968–1969 period.

Sviták, Ivan. *The Czechoslovak Experiment, 1968–1969*. New York: Columbia University Press, 1971.
A provocative, philosophical examination of the political events from the viewpoint of a critical Marxist thinker.

Tigrid, Pavel. *Why Dubček Fell*. London: Thomas Nelson & Sons, 1971.
An account of the crucial political maneuvering between the time of the Soviet intervention and the fall of Dubček (August 1968–April 1969).

Triska, Jan F. "Messages from Czechoslovakia." *Problems of Communism*, vol. 24, no. 6 (November–December 1975), pp. 26–42.
The beginnings of the dissent that led to the Charter 77 movement.

Valenta, Jiri. *Soviet Intervention in Czechoslovakia, 1968: Anatomy of a Decision*. Baltimore, Md.: Johns Hopkins University Press, 1969.
Sophisticated, systematic analysis of the Soviet foreign-policy process and the decision to intervene.

CULTURE

Chudoba, František. *A Short Survey of Czech Literature*. New York: E. P. Dutton & Co., 1929.
   An interesting outline of Czech literature up to the 1920s.

Hamšík, Dušan. *Writers Against Rulers*. London: Hutchinson & Co., and New York: Vintage Books, 1971.
   Insider's account of the 1967 writers' revolt.

Harkins, William E. *Anthology of Czech Literature*. New York: King's Crown Press, 1953.
   A selection of works culled from the long history of Czech writings.

Lamač, Miroslav. *Contemporary Art in Czechoslovakia*. Prague: Orbis, 1958.
   An illustrated survey of art, mostly from the first half of this century.

Liehm, Antonin J. *Closely Watched Films*. White Plains, N.Y.: International Arts and Sciences Press, 1974.
   A collection of interviews with many of the top Czech and Slovak film artists of the 1960s.

_____. *The Politics of Culture*. New York: Grove Press, 1973.
   Interviews with famous writers. Fascinating introductory chapters by Liehm and Jean-Paul Sartre.

Selver, Paul. *Czechoslovak Literature: An Outline*. London: Allen & Unwin, 1942.
   Very brief but useful as an overview of both Czech and Slovak literary traditions.

Šíp, Ladislav. *An Outline of Czech and Slovak Music*. Prague: Orbis, 1960.
   Musical traditions are traced back to their national origins.

Slovak Folk Art. 2 vols. Prague: Artia, 1964.
   A thorough and colorful work on the subject.

Wellek, René. *Essays on Czech Literature*. The Hague: Mouton, 1963.
   A sophisticated collection of writings on Czech literature and literary criticism by an eminent European scholar.

Wirth, Zdeněk, comp. *Czechoslovak Art from Ancient Times until the Present Day*. Prague: Orbis, 1926.
   Brief text with illustrative plates.

Index

Date Due